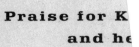

By the same author

100 Things I Hate About Pregnancy

About the Author

Kate Konopicky is the author of two books and a regular contributor to *Junior* magazine. She lives with her family in South Ealing, London.

A Woman of No Importance

Kate Konopicky

Vermilion
LONDON

1 3 5 7 9 10 8 6 4 2

First published in 2004 by Vermilion,
an imprint of Ebury Press, Random House,
20 Vauxhall Bridge Road, London SW1V 2SA
www.randomhouse.co.uk
This edition published in 2005

Random House Australia (Pty) Limited
20 Alfred Street, Milsons Point, Sydney,
New South Wales 2061, Australia

Random House New Zealand Limited
18 Poland Road, Glenfield,
Auckland 10, New Zealand

Random House South Africa (Pty) Limited
Endulini, 5A Jubilee Road,
Parktown 2193, South Africa

The Random House Group Limited Reg. No. 954009

Extract from 'This Be the Verse' from *High Windows* by Philip Larkin reproduced by permission of Faber & Faber Ltd

Papers used by Vermilion are natural, recyclable products made from wood grown in sustainable forests.

Printed and bound by Cox & Wyman Ltd, Reading, Berkshire

A CIP catalogue record for this book
is available from the British Library

ISBN 0-09-189864-1

Contents

Chapter One

A mother's place is in the wrong

Children begin by loving their parents.
After a time they judge them. Rarely, if ever,
do they forgive them.

Oscar Wilde, *A Woman of No Importance*

MY DAUGHTER IS FIVE NOW. FIVE GOING ON fifteen. It's been an interesting five years, packed with incident and achievement and the slow and sometimes painful blossoming of an ignorant and unformed lump of flesh into an almost normal human being. I'm talking about myself, naturally. Almost anybody can learn to walk and talk – some people (including small girls, unfortunately) can even chew gum at the same time. It's easy to be somebody's daughter. It takes courage, determination, blood, sweat, tears, a modicum of brute force and sheer dumb luck to get the hang of being somebody's mother. That, and the fact that you're not allowed to exchange the goods if they don't suit you. When I was pregnant I was planning on a compliant, thoughtful child with a constantly sunny disposition – I was going to be its mother, so what could it possibly have to complain about? When the child arrived it certainly didn't take five years, in fact it barely took five minutes, to realise that almost all of the things that I'd planned when I was pregnant were complete bollocks. Including doing fifty sit-ups every day and not wearing leggings. I had wondered about the strange silences that used to descend on friends with children when I was banging on about how I was going to carry on doing free-lance work when the baby was born and of course I couldn't possibly countenance building up my own landfill mountain with all those hateful disposable nappies. They didn't disabuse me of my foolish notions, they knew there was no point. They just let me carry on talking rubbish with all the confident ignorance of the childless. Bastards.

Not very long afterwards, while I was running around with my stomach hanging over the top of my leggings, busily filling skips with smelly nappies, it dawned on me that it is possible to be totally besotted with something you don't entirely understand. I was responsible for something that had even more complicated workings than a photocopier and it simply isn't true that a 'mother's instincts' will carry you through the baby equivalent of a paper jam. This was going to be a tad more challenging than I had thought.

For example. Imagine that you are really, really tired and somebody offers you a comfortable bed, soft lighting, a soothing atmosphere and the option of a little light supper before retiring. What do you do? Presumably you don't burst into tears (unless it's the sobs of gratitude to which the bone-weary are so prone if you show them a little kindness). Given the same set of circumstances, however, a small baby will see it as the perfect opportunity for a fit of uncontrollable weeping.

'She's tired,' friends would murmur sagely when deafened by my bawling daughter. 'Why doesn't she go to sleep then?' was my invariable, and I think quite reasonable, question. Nobody was ever able to give me a reasonable answer. It was this perverse behaviour that convinced me that, if men are from Mars and women are from Venus, babies are from an as yet unknown universe.

Baby faces are, we are told, designed to press all sorts of buttons in the adult brain, which immediately reduce it to mush. 'Aah, isn't she sweet!' is apparently the correct response when presented with an unfocused and dribble-spattered baby glare. It's a clever mechanism that the brain adopts to prevent it from dwelling on the fact that babies are incredibly badly behaved. Given the fact that they are totally dependent on adults, you would think that they would play it safe and try to be accommodating. On the contrary, they do everything in their tiny power to drive their parents to a pitch of hysteria and exhaustion that is a gnat's whisker away from total insanity. After a couple of weeks with a small baby almost anybody is capable of putting a nappy on its head and trying to feed the wrong end. (Ever wondered where the expression 'arse about tit' comes from? Think on.) Driving your parents into madness is normal baby behaviour. As a survival technique, frankly it would have had Darwin pausing to reconsider. As an alien plot to reduce the human race to sobbing jellies ripe for takeover, I think you'll find it makes perfect sense.

Once this thought was lodged in my brain the evidence started to mount. Even having spent nine months nurturing a small being inside my body, once she was on the outside it took me a while to get used to the fact of having brought another life into the world – let alone into our home. Just when I thought I had my life back to something like normality (i.e., spending all my waking hours feeding the loud end and cleaning the smelly end), Mr Colic came knocking at the door. Smashed it down with an axe, in fact. The yells were piteous and the poor helpless baby had even more helpless parents. She cried, I cried, her father's bottom lip was trembling visibly – I decided there must be something

I could do to help her. So like a well-behaved new mother, I asked the health visitor. Her reply simply staggered me. 'Yes, well, nobody really knows what colic is, but it could be that babies' guts are not fully developed and they have difficulty digesting.' What? *What?* They have nine months, for God's sake, which they fritter away forming ten tiny fingers and ten tiny toes which serve no useful purpose at all except for poking themselves in the eye and causing simpering relatives to coo 'Ooh, look at her little hands!' Small babies don't do much else except eat and sleep, so wouldn't it have been a good idea to get that equipment sorted out first? Two things, just *two things* that they are capable of doing and they are really useless at both. Of course, it could be that Mother Nature, hysterical with laughter at the huge joke that is baby and birth canal ('This'll make their eyes water! Hoo hoo hoo!') simply forgot to finish that bit off, but my theory of a race of alien invaders seemed more logically sound.

It was just a passing fancy, but in the early days with a small baby passing fancies can reach gigantic proportions in the befuddled parental brain. She was our daughter and we loved her passionately, but she was also a completely alien being.

As she grew I wearied of her flat refusal of delicious and nourishing earth food and watched with resignation as she pounced gleefully on cardboard, tissue paper and dead beetles, stuffing them all down her maw with apparently no ill effects. She would ignore doting aunts but form fierce attachments to egg boxes and video recorders – obviously things that reminded her of the folks back home.

A little chill would pass down my spine every time I noticed the secret messages passing between her and other babies as their prams crossed on the street. It may look, to the uninitiated, as if they are just eyeing up the opposition, but I was convinced that there was real communication between them. God help us if they ever get organised.

Before I got to grips with the situation she had a damn good try at sucking my brains out, too. I admit that I've spent most of my life talking crap, but it wasn't until I gave birth that I started talking *about* it.

Above all it was her weird sense of humour that nearly had me beat. A full half-hour of my best repertoire of funny faces and comic songs elicited no more than an unblinking stare of deep incomprehension – as if I was the one who was from another planet, for crying out loud. And yet the single act of wrapping a towel round my head brought on a fit of hysterical giggling. Putting a sponge in my mouth was simply the last word in comedy. And retrieving a toy from where it had been wilfully thrust down the side of the sofa had her practically slapping her thighs and wiping away the tears of laughter. Why was it funny when I cut my toenails? I longed to ask her, but by the time she could answer I had succeeded in clearing my first major parental hurdle.

Thanks to me she had undergone the Change and was now a member of the human race – all memories of her home planet obliterated. We could communicate, interact. We knew things about each other. We understood each other (up to a point). Obviously the workings of her little brain are still a complete mystery to me, but we do regard her as a real member of the family now. It's only occasionally, when I catch that faraway look in her eyes, that I still get a *frisson* and wonder whether I will ever truly know her. And whether I would truly want to, frankly.

But it was good. Eventually I knew I had a daughter, and not just an incomprehensible bundle of demands. With this minor triumph under my belt I began to feel as if I might be on the way to getting a handle on this mothering lark. But meanwhile, in the early months while I was still having my brains sucked out I noticed that not many people rushed to haul me back into the adult world of crackling wit and laser-like brainpower that I had been so used to. I still had to rejoin the human race myself. Becoming a mother seemed to have involved a subtle change in status. What am I saying? There was bugger all subtle about it. I imagine it must be like becoming old (and I'll soon find out if I'm right). Suddenly you are no longer a useful member of society helping turn the wheels of commerce but simply a drain on the resources of all the stockbrokers and bank managers who are, let's face it, the ones who matter. I suppose it didn't help that I was too tired to follow logical thought processes and I couldn't blame people for having low expectations of somebody who spent long hours pushing a pram round the streets, dressed in dirty clothes and carpet slippers and singing quietly. Replace the contents of the pram with a couple of tins of cat food and I think even I would have given myself a wide berth. Nevertheless, it would have been nice not to be dismissed out of hand as a tedious lamebrain.

At first I found it irritating, but after a while I used to look forward to being asked 'What do you do?' I positively enjoyed answering placidly 'Housewife and mother' and sat back to watch the panic rising as they mentally ran through and rejected all the stock answers. 'Does it pay well?' Perhaps not. 'Oh, my brother does that.' Not desperately likely. 'How interesting.' Dear God, no.

Then relief would strike in a visible wave as they hit on the only possible answer. 'Oh, most important job in the world, that,' they would murmur unctuously before sloping off to find someone more interesting, like an accountant or a tax inspector. Everybody says it and nobody believes it, although, ironically, it is the most important job in the world and it's impossible to do it right. So, no pressure there, then.

We all know that the skills involved in being a parent are legion. In any paid employment it would euphemistically be called 'multi-tasking' (in other words, half your colleagues have been made redundant and somebody's got to do it). Within the confines of your home it's called 'not doing much at all really'. Any parent is a combination of teacher, nurse, nutritionist, psychologist, entertainer and mind reader. You don't get weekends off and you don't get to phone in sick when you fancy a lie-in. You get plenty of appraisals but precious little praise. The boss is illogical, impossible to reason with, incapable of undertaking the simplest task without rigid supervision and is prone to tantrums. Yes, I know we've all had jobs like that but at least we got paid for them.

Worst of all, however hard you work, whatever you do is wrong. I always thought of myself as intelligent, sensible, competent, firm in my opinions, patient and calm. It took the birth of my daughter to make me realise that I am in fact stupid, irritable, ham-fisted, lazy, illogical and have a tendency to cave in rather quickly to unreasonable demands. Trying to be a good mother is a bit like herding cats: one small victory is quickly overshadowed by a dozen glaringly obvious failures. If you go back to paid employ-ment you are neglecting your children at the most important time in their lives; if you give up work and stay at home your children will be clingy and shy and lack independence. It's not long before any mother with half a brain cell will do the only sensible thing and give up. You know you can't win.

Mistrust anyone who claims to be a good mother. She's

probably been reading books and getting ideas and is missing the point entirely – it simply can't be done. Her children will probably spend all their free time in houses where there is chocolate on tap and the TV is constantly switched to the cartoon channel, while she's at home wondering where her purse went and why they missed their violin lessons. Meanwhile the mother with the red-hot remote and the sticky soft furnishings will be reviled by her children because she never made them study the violin so they never had the opportunity to nurture their latent musical talents. Moreover, you must treat with open hostility any mother who pretends to be doing a better job than you are. If you are foolish enough to voice openly your anxieties about bedtime routines and some smug mumsy type starts suggesting you use her foolproof methods, just poke her in the eye with a night light. It might very well be true that her little Tom is fast asleep by seven o'clock prompt without fail, but what she is neglecting to mention is that during his waking hours he will only eat jam sandwiches and has a tendency towards kleptomania. If there's no such thing as the perfect mother, there's certainly no such thing as the perfect child.

It did take a while for this to sink in, however, so I wasted a lot of time trying to be a good mother before I realised that, like the true communist state, it only exists in theory. Nobody will admit it at first, of course, any more than you would ever hear them say 'Oh I'm an absolutely useless driver' or 'Actually I'm crap at sex'. Statistically, either or both of those two statements must be true of at least half the population, but everybody's keeping quiet about it. Similarly, we all have little setbacks on the parental road to perdition, but because you can't do it perfectly doesn't mean you can't do it at all. 'Yes, I tried accountancy but failed the exams so I chucked it in.' 'Mmm, with me it was motherhood.' You might feel like chucking it in sometimes and becoming a hermit, but it's not going to happen. You just have to get used to being in the wrong.

So there you are stuck, up to your armpits in 'the most important job in the world' and a little encouragement wouldn't go amiss. It's a bit like the way children never pick up good habits in the playground, only bad ones. Nobody ever says 'How clever of you to get her washed and fed and dressed in such a charming outfit – all before noon!' No, they are more likely to stare pointedly at the piles of dirty laundry and ask in a concerned tone of voice if you are coping all right. It starts when the baby is born and your own mother (who has a bloody short memory) starts telling you about things that 'never did you any harm' and is very free with her criticism of your parenting skills. This is bad enough, but then before you can say 'babywipes' you find yourself locking horns with a toddler who can barely speak but you are absolutely certain has the NSPCC on redial and will scream blue murder if you have the temerity to serve her juice in the wrong cup. 'But I wanted the *blue* one!' Any household with young children will soon be echoing with the parental wail: 'What? What? What have I done wrong now?' We all start off thinking that as long as you take time to reason with your children and explain everything calmly and logically then they will accept your superior knowledge and bow to your authority. Nothing wrong with that. Except – let me think now – 'children', 'reason', 'explain', 'calm', 'logic' and 'authority'. Given my previous reliance on logical argument, which seemed to work OK in the adult world, I was somewhat at a loss when faced with a fizzing ball of rage because I had suggested calmly and reasonably that it might be a good idea to put her shoes on before we went out on the street. Far from accepting my authority she was actually blaming me for it. At times like these 'Because I said so' seems like reasoning worthy of Wittgenstein.

Between the kid baying at me and the experts helpfully pointing out ten different ways to make the kid stop baying at me, is it any wonder that the phrase 'benign neglect' came to hold a haunting attraction. This way of thinking started even before she was old enough to have her own (ill-informed and ridiculous) opinions to challenge me with and hardened into steely-minded resolve as the months passed. I should stop trying to do things right and just do things. It was OK, I didn't have to rush out to HMV because we didn't have the right kind of Mozart to soothe the savage beast. (Yes, I do mean beast.) It really didn't matter if I was still in my dressing gown at noon, as long as she was well and happy. Why couldn't I pick her up when she was crying, if I wanted to? Surely three months was a little early to start instilling discipline? So what if I haven't washed her hair for over a week, it's not like she's going to any cocktail parties. And anyway, that little Hitleresque smear of fringe on her forehead is simply there as an antidote to all the babies who look like Winston Churchill. The more other people, books and childcare pundits told me what I should be doing, the more these rebellious thoughts just kept on popping into my head. Or was I just being a lousy mother again? Funny how steely-minded resolve can crumble into whimpering timidity whenever there's a child involved. Especially a cross one.

But God knows, should you ever falter in your determination to do the right thing, there are plenty of people queuing up to tell you how to do this 'most important job in the world'. You can read an instruction manual to tell you how to put the buggy together. A nice lady in John Lewis was very helpful in overlooking my incompetence with a nursing bra. Claim forms for maternity pay are relatively straightforward. Other books, guides written by fashionable gurus and kindly – yet malicious – relatives will be falling over themselves to tell you how to explain death or put a stop to nose-picking. It's probably best to keep the instruction book for the buggy but chuck all the rest of it on a bonfire, including the relatives (but not the nice lady from John Lewis). They're just guessing. Let's take as an example books and magazine articles on how to cook interesting and nutritious food for your toddler. I can't count the number of times I've read about making little food faces with peas for eyes and slivers of carrot for a smiley mouth. It's such fun the kids will just love it and gobble up their greens before you can say Sabatier! Hang on a minute, does that mean that if I'm intending to create two faces you expect me to cook four peas and two slices of carrot by themselves? Why of *course*. I'll stuff a mushroom while I'm at it, while counting the number of angels I can fit on a pinhead with the other hand. Or maybe you're assuming that the whole family eats together? Of course you are, because that's what perfect families do, except that if she needs feeding at five and Daddy doesn't get home until eight it doesn't really work. *Does it?* Besides which, the toddler brain being what it is, you can create an Arcimboldo on a plate, only to be told that she doesn't want to eat it because the man looks nice. At this point, cookbook goes out of the window and pizza goes into the oven – with all the green peppers picked off, naturally, in case she sullies her digestive system with something vaguely nutritious. It's all fine and dandy in theory but you can follow the rules religiously and still fail – as anyone knows who has done all the right things with a nit comb before discovering that a thumbnail works better.

I was beginning to formulate a conspiracy theory. The whole world, from dippy aunts to dingbat cookery writers and smug stockbrokers, was ganging up on me to tell me I was doing everything wrong. And yet I had a happy and healthy child. Social Services hadn't been called once. Not once. Perhaps – without the faintest nuance of complacency – just perhaps, I wasn't doing too badly. At the risk of getting cocky I thought I could safely ignore any advice I hadn't actually asked for and revel in my status as proper and confident mother. What I was experiencing was a bit like that one fine day in February that gives you the strength to go on because you know that spring will come at last. In fact, there's still an awful lot of crap to get through before the sun finally comes out. But there was the odd glimmer of light.

There's one question that guilt-ridden and anxious parents never ask themselves: 'If I'm so useless at this, how come I'm still feeling iffy about handing my best-beloved over to someone with 150 years' worth of childcare experience and qualifications coming out of her ears? Surely I should be overjoyed to offload the job on to someone whose sole purpose in life is to push buggies round parks and cook individual peas?' Could it be that, at the back of your mind, there's a tiny conviction that you are actually best placed to look after your own child? Once, when talking to a friend about the difficulties of finding suitable childcare, and having been made deeply despondent by the collection of lazy and grubby simpletons who were offering their services as childminders, I said that I wanted somebody as good as I was. 'Oh no,' she replied gloomily, 'I want somebody better than me.' Feeling guilty about her occasional peevish outbursts at her children and her inability to make a decent gingerbread man she was assuming that a professional could do the job better. Not so. Mary Poppins doesn't exist. (And even if she did, the waiting list would be so long you would have to put your grandchildren down while you were still in nappies yourself.) As a mother, you are as good as it gets. I had to admit that this might be faint comfort to my daughter when it finally dawned on her that I was her mother, drunk or sober, and her family would never be like the ones in the adverts, but maybe I could encourage her to look on the bright side. I would never make it as a TV mum, but at least she wouldn't have to drink Sunny Delight.

Coming to terms with my mediocrity as a mother was a massive relief. I joyously embraced the fact that as a family we were destined to be less like the Waltons and more like the Simpsons (or, quite possibly, the Addams). I could stop trying to be a perfect mother – I was only upsetting myself. Until the day when 'throwing the baby out with the bath water' took on a literal meaning for me, I could relax and just get on with it.

Relax? Who was I kidding? I'd started, but I wasn't ever going to finish. Are we there yet, Mummy? No, dear, nor are we ever likely to be.

Chapter Two

Don't you think you should...

ONCE THE INITIAL SHOCK IS OVER, BEING A family is rather nice. 'Nuclear' seems a bit of an unfortunate term for something so warm and cosy and wrapped up in itself. Or maybe it's called that because the fallout is so far-reaching. Privacy? Ability to make your own decisions? An enclosed and secluded home life? You can forget about all that as soon as the sperm hits the egg. It's not surprising I had doubts about my abilities as a mother when so many other people seemed to have an opinion on the matter.

I wouldn't dream of approaching a slender young woman totally unknown to me and remarking 'Thinking of getting pregnant? Would you prefer a boy or a girl?' No more would I comment to any man with a stomach the size of triplets, 'Blimey, I bet you had to drink a lot of beer to get that.' But it seemed to me that all I had to do to attract the unwanted attention of every Nosy Parker on the street (not all of them entirely sober, in my experience) was to walk about being pregnant. I know that people think they are expressing a friendly interest, and perhaps I'm just a cantankerous old bag, but I really, *really* hated it. And however much I wanted to say 'I don't know you from Adam and my private life is none of your business', I was forced by my upbringing to reply politely. 'No, I don't know if it's a boy or a girl. No, we don't mind as long as it's healthy. No, we haven't decided on a name. Please go away now.' I wish I'd had the front to look these people straight in the eye and say grimly, 'I'm not pregnant. It's dropsy.' I never did, but I began to regret never having attended self-assertiveness classes. And I'd need a Ph.D. in one-upmanship in order to get through to some people.

And if pregnancy made me subject to unwanted attention, the outcome was even worse. I don't even like to remember the circus that was childbirth. At the time I was in no position to think about my modesty, but there's something utterly demeaning about being poked about by strangers while losing control of your bodily functions and uttering a sort of bovine lowing sound. A beautiful experience? Not really. A private joy? Joy, yes; private, no.

I like my privacy. I could never understand people who complained about the anonymity of London and how awful it was not to be intimate with your neighbours. This was a major advantage of London life as far as I was concerned. I had absolutely no desire to be chummy with people just because they lived in the flat above or below me – saying hello over the dustbins was quite enough for me. I also remember a friend who was brought up in a small village bemoaning the fact that when he was a teenager he couldn't have half a cider and a Woodbine without his parents finding out about it within five minutes. It tended to cramp his style a little. Now we're a family and we live in a house I understand exactly what he meant. From being a carefree singleton happy to plough my own furrow I am now living the same way my parents did. We are part of a community, like it or not. I can't walk from the tube to my front door without exchanging greetings with at least one or two people – and they're usually under ten years old.

There used to be a couple who lived a few doors away with whom we became friendly, mostly because our children were the same age. Deborah was my main source of local knowledge (gossip) when we moved in and I was soon up to speed on street scandals, when one day she mentioned that she and her husband had lived on that street for years and not known anyone at all – until they had children. Being a parent is so unpleasantly public. I also suspect that if I am privy to gossip about several of my neighbours then they must know more about us than I would normally care to divulge. I've taken to carrying my empties down the road to the bottle bank because I am sure one of my neighbours counts the bottles in our recycling box. Obviously it's great for our daughter to be an accepted part of the social circle of the playground, but if I'm honest I'd rather be totally anonymous. I'm not even immune from the local kids. We all bang on about how wonderfully curious children are about everything, but being on the receiving end can get a little wearing. I'm tired of having to justify my choice of soft furnishings to an eight-year-old ('Why have you got a blue sofa? It's not the same as ours') or being greeted with a chorus of 'Where ya going?' from the gaggle of kids clustered around the gate whenever I leave the house. 'Out! I'm going out! Mind your own business and leave me alone!' Come to think of it, there's no perhaps about it: I *am* a cantankerous old bag.

It started in earnest as soon as I returned home from hospital with my precious bundle. A home that was suddenly filled with a stream of visitors who didn't really do much except dirty all the cups. And although I was very grateful for the help of midwives and health visitors in the early days, I couldn't help feeling I was under surveillance. Which I was, of course, and I had to quash my faint feelings of resentment that they had to check that I wasn't dangerous or neglectful. The very idea! I was surprised they felt they had to ask. But I did think I had gained the trust of our health visitor when she admitted that she didn't drink tea when she was working because she found that other people's toilets were often not of the cleanest. 'No! Really? You can have a tour of our toilet any time you like – no need to give notice.' She declined, but I felt a minor glow of victory. There you are, you can tell me I'm not holding the baby properly but at least my toilet can stand up to scrutiny.

Those days are gone but general nosiness hasn't. I'm thinking of changing my hairdresser because I'm sick of her quizzing me about when my daughter is going to get a little brother or sister. Perfectly nice woman, but she's my hairdresser for God's sake. She knows nothing about my life or circumstances but should at least have noticed the state of my hair, considering her profession. I didn't dye it that grey – perhaps that should suggest something to her. But no, she keeps twittering on about two being better than one, and only children really need someone else to play with, while I squirm and mutter vaguely about 'letting nature take its course'. Not mentioning that the next thing that nature has in store for me is probably the menopause. It's all a bit intrusive and a little upsetting – and she missed a bit of fringe last time.

At least the hairdresser can lay claim to knowing me a little. Mad old women at bus stops have no excuse for inflicting their unwanted opinions on us. Stand quietly with a small child and you're laying yourself open to criticism.

One woman in particular is lodged in my memory. She started by questioning me closely about my daughter, whether she liked school, if she had to wear a uniform and so on, before turning on the girl, who, to her credit, fixed the old bat with a baleful glare and refused to answer her impertinent questions. So I got the full force of her lecture on the sheer awfulness of the youth of today, and the feck-lessness of modern parents, and how rude it was not to answer when somebody asked you a question. I must say I was with my daughter on this one – I think it's incredibly rude to subject a complete stranger to an interrogation on their parenting decisions, but I was far too polite to say 'No, of course she doesn't play truant you ridiculous old trout, she's five years old.' I just had to stand there and take it while my lips disappeared into a thin line of resentment. Would she have grilled a middle-aged man about his business ethics? I think not, but as a mother and child we were fair game.

Obviously that woman was as mad as a fish, but it wasn't so very different from the barrage of advice and criticism that lands on you with all the subtlety of an ava-lanche as soon as you become a parent.

What is it about having a child that makes everyone think they know better than you do? Is this some unspoken social contract that I wasn't told about – the mere fact of turning up on your doorstep with an ugly and unsuitable present gives people the right to start lecturing? You can, if you choose to, quite successfully ignore all books, television programmes and *Woman's Hour*, but when face to face with people it seems impossible to escape the flood of advice that comes in all forms from the mildly irritating to the downright lunatic.

During the first three months of my daughter's life alone, I was told that she looked like a boy and I should dress her in pink; that in temperatures rising 30°C she ought to have socks on; that she was thirsty and needed a little fruit juice (this was at two weeks old – it probably would have killed her); and I was exhorted to give her formula milk as soon as possible because breast-feeding is bad for you. I happen not to like baby powder. I think it's messy and unnecessary and I didn't want my lovely daughter to have a claggy bum. But I was wrong about that, too, apparently. After listening to thousands of sentences that all begin 'Don't you think you should…' I developed a glazed look – a glaze which soon hardened into an unbreakable carapace, to protect me from the danger of collapsing under the weight of all that 'well-meant' (ha!) advice.

My favourite piece of advice, though, was given to a friend of mine. She was told, quite seriously, by her mother-in-law that she must on no account give her son baby massage because it would turn him into a homosexual.

(Mind you, I only think it's funny because it didn't happen to me. Her husband still goes pink when I remind him of it. Which is often.)

And then there are the people who insist they have 'a way' with children. I quite often had my crying daughter plucked from my protective grasp by somebody who was convinced that the best way to quiet a hungry baby is to jiggle it up and down and sing. I'm no expert on babies but I can make an educated guess that when a baby cries it's not *often* because it's suddenly developed a yen to be bounced up and down and cooed at by a complete stranger. Although, of course I could be wrong about that as well.

It was of no consequence that my child was healthy and happy, apparently not worthy of comment that the person ladling out the advice last had a kid forty years ago and he was brought up by a nanny; no matter that her children have turned out to be complete sociopaths; and totally irrelevant that I spent quite a bit of time with my child and just might know her a little better than someone who called round for half an hour. People just wouldn't shut up. But at least the sort of interference I was subjected to never impinged too much on my life. How's this for a story? A craftswoman building up her own business was interviewed by a national newspaper about her life. The printed interview made it clear that sometimes her twelve-year-old daughter had to make her own breakfast while her mother did an early shift at a local job. The result was a series of abusive emails to the woman accusing her of not being a fit mother, and finally a visit from the police. This is absolutely true, and rather chilling.

None of those people who were so ready with their accusations knew anything about that mother and daughter and how they lived their lives, but parenting is something on which everyone has an opinion. Just as everyone who can read thinks they can write, everyone who has ever been a child thinks they know the best way to bring one up. The only foolproof way to bring up a child is to eat it first. Otherwise it rather depends. It depends on you, on the child, on your circumstances – on hundreds of variables – and I don't think being dogmatic about it is very helpful. Even deciding on your own rules without interference can land you on very shaky ground.

Some rules are set in stone and can always be relied on: always wash your hands after going to the toilet (unless you work in catering or the NHS, obviously); never let the dog lick your plate. But when I was formulating my own set of household regulations I was surprised at how often I seemed to confuse 'always' with 'never'. For example.

- 'Always/never listen to the child's requests and bear in mind that she has rights and opinions, too.' That's easy, it's 'always', obviously. Isn't it?

Or should she just learn to do as she's told
because Mother knows best and she's still too
young to know what's good for her? Maybe it's
'sometimes' – which makes for a rather
inconsistent rule so I might as well scrap that
one and play it by ear. Let's try another one.

- 'When going out with a toddler and a buggy
  always/never carry everything with you that you
  might possibly need.' Again, I started off
  thinking it was 'always' until I realised that I
  would end up needing a pantechnicon for every
  short trip to the shops, so I would stick to
  essentials and developed a flair for
  improvisation. But then again, it does depend
  how far you are going and for how long …

- 'Always/never explain everything in detail.' Of
  course I would never dream of fobbing my
  daughter off with vague and meaningless replies
  to difficult questions – until she asked one.

- 'Always/never make rigid rules that cannot be
  broken.'

By this time I was beginning to see which way the wind was
blowing and decided that, apart from basic rules regarding
hygiene and dangerous stunts I was probably going to
spend quite a lot of my parenting life simply busking it.

Maybe that was why other people were so free with their opinions on how I should bring up my child. It's easy and probably deeply satisfying to dish out advice when you don't have to put it into practice yourself.

But I have to admit that among all the lunatic stuff I did receive some helpful and practical suggestions from people who'd been through it all themselves. When our daughter was born, friends who already had children rallied round with muslin squares and cast-off clothes and tried *not* to act as if they were welcoming me into a secret society. Friends without children just didn't get it. I know they didn't because I experienced exactly the same sort of benign incomprehension of new mothers before I became one myself. Of course, not having children never stopped anybody having theories about them, most of them extremely judgmental. Try as you may, you will never live up to their high (theoretical) standards. Other parents I have spoken to have all come to the same conclusion: paying a visit to childless homes with a small but mobile child of your own in tow is simply not worth the trouble.

One thing that's even worse than going to see friends with children and spending the entire time talking about kids is going to see friends without children and spending the entire time apologising. First of all, people without children live in nice houses (or 'deathtraps' as I like to think of them). 'No, that's fine,' your friends keep repeating (with a little less conviction every time) as you try to carry on a normal adult conversation while grabbing the corners of the glass coffee table, prising first editions out of grubby fingers and surreptitiously trying to remove orange juice from the sofa with a hankie dipped in spit. They have probably imagined their house filled with a few artistically scattered toys and the sounds of childish laughter. You, meanwhile, are imagining a trail of destruction of which the Vikings might have been proud. (That's probably a little hard on the Vikings – a cultured and thoughtful people, apparently, which you couldn't say about children, unless you count 'plotting' as 'thinking'.) Two-year-olds just won't sit quietly doing a jigsaw while the adults talk over their heads. People without personal knowledge of small children simply can't understand why not. They reason that an adult should have complete control over a small child, much as you can control a dog. If a dog misbehaves it's because you haven't trained it properly; *ergo*, if a child 'misbehaves' you must be an inadequate parent and just not doing your job properly. Any parent knows that while you are in charge of a toddler there is nothing else in the room, or even the world, that's going to get your full attention. But I've been with people who have been visibly irritated when their conversation is interrupted and I was clearly not hanging on their every word because I was called on every five minutes to provide drinks, wipe a nose, rub a bruise or find a toy. What did they expect? That's what you are faced with if you take a small child to visit a childless couple – total mutual misunderstanding.

I suspected that a particular couple of childless friends had secretly been grooming themselves into the roles of favourite auntie and uncle – the jolly, indulgent ones that the kids just adore – after all, they could have all the enjoyment and hand the kid back after a few hours of childish fun. When it came to putting it into practice, however, they hadn't a clue how to entertain a small child and I spent the afternoon frantically trying to find some way of saving a doomed friendship and stopping jolly auntie from booting my kid up the backside in a fit of rage.

I can remember sitting with people who were under the impression that I was exactly the same as I used to be, with a miniature version of myself tagging along, trying to talk intelligently about films I hadn't seen and books I hadn't read, while on my side of the room a growing sense of inadequacy loomed like a cloud and on the other side of the room they could only just stop their nostrils flaring with disappointment and distaste. 'Why can't they just *stop* her spilling juice?' they were thinking, then realisation dawned and I could see them making mental notes never to sit on my sofa again without protective clothing. But however much of a struggle it may be, it's always better to talk about books you haven't read than try to explain what it's like

living with a child. In an unguarded moment I once mentioned to a then childless friend that I got fed up with picking
up after my daughter and tripping over her toys. 'Doesn't
she have a room of her own with all her toys in it?' she
asked. 'Of course, but she brings them downstairs and
leaves them all over the place.' 'Oh, I'd be terribly strict
about that,' she retorted quickly. With one phrase she had
managed to make me feel like a weak and over-indulgent
mother with no sense of discipline because I let my daughter
play with toys outside the confines of her bedroom. I
supposed she would be terribly strict about orange juice on
the sofa as well, but I had long since come to the conclusion
that I could either spend my entire life being terribly strict
or wash the sofa covers occasionally while my child learned
to cope with drinking from a cup. I soon made my choice –
and if that meant buying a new sofa it didn't make me a bad
mother. Just a bone-idle spendthrift.

But in a situation like this, once the breakdown in communication starts it's not going to get any better. My friends
had already started revising their opinions of me, and every
thought began with the words 'No child of mine would
ever...' Hopeless to explain that 'Yes, every child of yours
would...' because they simply wouldn't have believed me.
And the moment I really needed my child to be cute and
adorable and well-behaved I knew exactly what she was
going to do. On one particularly sticky afternoon (in more

ways than one) at the home of friends I could see the storm clouds gathering but in my state of heightened anxiety was powerless to disperse them. In someone else's house the sort of tantrum that at home can either be diverted or ignored reaches operatic proportions – and I'm talking Wagner. At home it would have been a mild irritation, but under the withering gaze of people who by now regarded me as an incompetent fool I was reduced to a quivering jelly while my daughter grew horns and a tail and screamed herself sick. Quite literally. (And nobody thanked me for catching it in my hands. Incompetent? I think not – it wasn't me who tried to serve chicken with chillies to a two-year-old.)

People without children don't understand – but they don't understand that they don't understand, and nothing will convince them otherwise. Except one thing. On the way home from that disastrous afternoon I calculated that even if my friend got pregnant the very next day it would be ages before I could start my really serious gloating. The day did come, I'm glad to say, although when I first met her little boy he was so well-behaved I was tempted to stick pins in him. It wasn't until he was about two that I was a gleeful witness to his bad temper. I must remember to ask my friend if she's terribly strict about toys all over the house – or could I be that cruel? Yes, I think I probably could.

So after years of feeling I was public property I've

become accustomed to the scrutiny of other people and highly sensitive to every nuance of criticism or disapproval. I've also learned to ignore it. I know exactly who thinks I am a useless mother, even though they won't actually say it to my face. But I know I'm not that useless so they can talk about me behind my back if they like, and I'm not going to take any notice. If you never really know what goes on in other families there's a very good reason for it. It's none of your business.

Chapter Three

Change: it's not just for nappies

THOSE CHILDLESS FRIENDS OF OURS JUST HADN'T grasped the fundamental nature of what had happened to us. We had barely grasped it ourselves, but life was certainly different with a baby. Game over. We were parents now, so had to put away childish things (in all senses, unless one of us wanted to break a hip tripping over them) and kiss our freedom goodbye. Although I will admit to having daft ideas when I was pregnant, I was never one of those women who maintain that their child will have to fit in with its parents' schedules and they have no intention of giving up any aspect of their busy and exciting lives. If that's your attitude you might as well get a hamster. At least they don't need babysitters and anyway they don't last that long (especially if stepped on). Of course I was expecting things to change, everybody keeps telling you things are going to change in that annoying way that people have of saying 'You won't know what's hit you, of course, until it does.' And they were right, which is even more annoying. Birth is like death: nothing prepares you for it. It doesn't matter whether you are stocking up on swaddling clothes or winding sheets, when the event happens there aren't many people who can simply take it in their stride and carry on as normal.

I can't blame the child entirely for my altered view of the world. I've long since said goodbye to my hot youth (although I understand he's doing quite well in the City now) so it's not surprising that I quite like being at home, and would probably quite like being at home whether there was a small girl living there or not. I used to wake up on a sunny Sunday and think 'Hooray, it's a lovely day – we can go and have a drink by the river.' Now I wake up on a sunny Sunday and think 'Hooray, it's a lovely day – I can get three loads of washing dry.' (Except I don't think 'Hooray', exactly.) So of course I have changed, except that while I am pegging out socks I would still quite *like* to be swilling lager and getting my shoulders singed. Maybe my bone-idle pleasure seeking character is still there, it has just been subsumed under the weight of tedious responsibilities. And let's face it, unless you are Peter Stringfellow, the pleasures of youth do tend to pall after a while and the siren call of the cocoa mug seems very appealing, although you never think it's going to happen to you. If, once, some hooded figure had sidled up to me in a Soho bar while I was being all brittle and modern and whispered 'This very night fifteen years hence will find you crawling about in undergrowth with a torch and a blunt instrument' I would have scoffed, frankly. Probably pooh-poohed as well. Not just at the idea that I was destined to spend my Friday nights killing slugs, but also that it would actually be important to me in years to come. Nowadays I would rather be clubbed than go clubbing (unless it's slug-clubbing, of course), but I can't use parenthood as an excuse for my reluctance to stand around in smoky bars parting with tenners quicker than a drunken gambler. All those skinny young things with ugly hairstyles advertising strong drink and unwearable clothes don't know it yet, but there will come a day when each and every one of them will find themselves in a supermarket seriously pondering the relative merits of toilet cleaners. You see if I'm not right. But I do like to think that when the weight of tedious responsibilities has lightened a little I shall not just slip into my slippers but have a whale of a time being drunk in charge of a bus pass. We'll see.

While we're on the subject of time passing, what the hell did I do with it all before I had a child? Before the baby was born I must have had aeons of the stuff in which to read books, file my nails, meet friends for drinks, even sleep for more than two hours at a stretch. Then all at once time was no longer a fixed continuum. The nature of a minute, an hour, a day or a year suddenly became flexible. My first realisation of this came to me when my daughter was only a couple of weeks old and I found myself in the shower at two o'clock in the afternoon thinking with my fuzzy brain, 'If I've been up since five, how come I haven't managed to *do* anything all day?' Pre-motherhood, I probably could have cleaned the house, done the laundry and cooked a delicious meal (well, a meal anyway), given that number of waking hours at home. Add a baby to the domestic set-up and clocks become meaningless. When her father came home and asked me how my day was I was stumped for an answer. 'Was that a whole day? I managed to put a wash on while she was asleep but it's still in the machine because I didn't have time to take it out.' *I didn't have time!* It's not physically possible but it happens. Baby-time is a special case, admittedly, but toddler-time is almost as bad. The joy of seeing the first wobbly steps was soon replaced by the realisation that a baby is at least containable. Once they're up on their legs you have to watch them every minute so I spent a great deal of time during those years not doing anything except acting as a sort of guard dog. Put a small child in a paddling pool and that's it, you might as well be chained to it until such time as the child gets bored or cold (which can be quite a long time to sit and be splashed at).

I wouldn't like to add up the hours of my life I have spent in playgrounds, simply patrolling. It would probably amount to time I could have spent on a round-the-world cruise or building the Eiffel Tower in matchsticks. I couldn't even read a book in case I was suddenly called on to perform a spectacular save. I suppose it was good for my daughter to learn how to climb, jump and slide without major mishap and I knew I was doing the right thing, but at the end of another of those tedious days in the park I couldn't help thinking guiltily 'God, what a waste of time.'

At five she is quite capable now of looking after herself to a certain extent (usually to the extent of switching on a video), but I suspect that I might have overdone the one-to-one care in the early years, because she still seems to expect it. I still wonder what I used to do with my evenings and weekends before *somebody* needed feeding, bathing, fairy stories, trips to the cinema or the Science Museum, urgent help with bottom-wiping or a partner for snakes and ladders. We got her a cat, but he's completely useless at all of the above activities so it still means my time is not my own. Even when I can persuade them to play together I am constantly called to be a witness to his amusing behaviour when I would far rather be reading the paper. When she has a friend round to play they deliberately devise games that require three players, just in case I find something better to do than turn skipping ropes or count to a hundred while they hide.

And child-time is just as freakish as baby-time. Usually, if you say 'Just a minute' to someone's request for your attention, it is a signal for them to wait for a few seconds while you complete building a tower of champagne glasses or put the finishing touches to a basket of spun sugar before giving them your full consideration. If I try saying it to my daughter I am met with loud complaints that I'm taking about a hundred minutes and the expectation that I should drop everything and speed to her side immediately. Two seconds takes too long. And if I do rush to answer her plaintive calls it's usually because she wants me to see her favourite bit in a video. 'It's a video. I can watch it again. That's the point. Can I get back to blackleading the grate, now?' (Yes, I was using the video as a babysitter. Do you want to make something of it?) The only advantage to this strange alteration in timescales is that it has taught me to appreciate time. I appreciate it so much I just wish I had more of it. That took time as well, of course. One of the most important rites of passage in the first five years of my daughter's life was the first day at the playgroup. I've no idea what she thought about it: all I knew was I had an hour and a half to myself to spend as I wished and I didn't know what to do with it. Unfortunately the sense of freedom went to my head and I frittered the time away doing housework when I could have been reading a book, or indeed writing one. I know better now, of course, but you should see the state of the kitchen floor.

While all this weird chronology stuff was going on I noticed a change in how I regarded myself. I was somebody's mother. Naturally I tried hard to ignore the weight of that particular responsibility lest it crushed me entirely, but it kept on nagging at me. Was I a different person? Surely not. It's not me that's changed, it's just I have different things to do. And different things to think about. I don't believe I'm the only person who has looked into the face of a two-day-old baby and started planning education, fashion tips, advice on skin care, what to do about unsuitable boyfriends and how to explain sex. With all these castles in the air came the embarrassing remembrance of all the appalling things I did to my mother when I was a child, and the horrible realisation that my daughter would do exactly the same to me and never understand what she was doing until she had children of her own. I saw a vast unending cycle of children and parents locked in a pattern of misunderstanding and selfish demands on each other that would carry on for all time. And she was still only two days old. This was not a cheering image to dwell on, especially for someone new to the job. I vowed that whatever changed and whatever stayed the same, at least I could break that vicious circle and not turn into my own mother. A vow made by every other new mother in the world, I imagine. If nothing else, parenthood can probably be defined as one enormous cliché.

But I wasn't the only one who had been thrust into parenthood. The child had a father as well, and all the kindly manuals will gently point out that you might find that your relationship will undergo some adjustment. This might be a good thing. You might find that, instead of having the same old arguments about toilet cleaning or socks on the floor, you will find other subjects to squabble about, viz: who has had the least sleep. 'I'm tired!' 'You're tired! How do you think I feel?' and so on until you wake the baby up. A good example of the complete idiocy of the phrase 'a change is as good as a rest'. Mostly you are advised, when spoiling for a fight, to 'sit down and talk about it. Tell him how you feel.' More complete idiocy. It's the last thing you should do, especially when you are in a boiling rage because of something your partner has done or hasn't done. Tell him how you feel at a moment like that and they'll know about it in Sydney. I freely admit that I'm not much given to picking over the bones of a relationship and I don't do soul-searching conversations. We just sort of get on with it, and when I read in another of those kindly manuals that sometimes new fathers may feel excluded or neglected and I should be careful to take his feelings into consideration my reaction was something along the lines of 'Tough.' In case you are still under any illusions, I would like to point out that this is not a kindly advice manual.

But you are sharing a 'wonderful' new experience and

it can lead to the discovery of previously unknown skills in your partner. Breast-feeding isn't usually one of them, unfortunately, but adroitness with a bottle comes in very handy, whether he's feeding the baby or doling out the gin. He turns 'to burp' from a distressingly loud personal foible into a transitive verb. Marvellous! And when a man previously known for his wicked sarcasm suddenly displays a proficiency for slapstick, it is nothing short of stupendous, as long as it's temporary and confined to the nursery. Finding new and useful personality traits in each other is all to the good. More disturbing may be the discovery of previously unknown opinions and beliefs, such as an aversion to/insistence on severe haircuts, or the stock of home remedies that have lain forgotten at the back of his mind until he finds a reason to dust them off and inflict them on your ailing child. 'Your mother used to put *what* on a graze?'

But the new skills that are foisted upon you can come as a surprise. I've always left engineering to clever people, which is why it took me several hours of practice, while heavily pregnant, to work out how to fold a buggy. The more practised mother I had bought it from assured me it was possible to do it with one hand, but I couldn't see how it could be managed with less than three. I did get the hang of it in the end, to the extent of being so blasé about it that I would regularly abuse it (in direct contradiction to the instructions) and hang heavy shopping bags on the handles.

It tipped up one day and in catching it I tore a ligament in my thumb so badly I saw stars. I didn't remember childbirth hurting that much. However practised I was in buggy-pushing, I evidently still wasn't that skilled.

Among all the shifts in relationships, responsibilities, time zones and world order there is the more prosaic nature of the physical changes you are forced to undergo – not many of them good. Not any of them good. Unless you count the ability to go without sleep as a life-enhancing accomplishment. Which I don't. When my daughter was about three I saw a fascinating television programme about what happens to your body when you are pregnant. It made me sick to my stomach – which was apparently exactly what happened when my unborn daughter had grown big enough to squash all my internal organs into a space not big enough to accommodate a bowl of cornflakes. But after nine months of sucking me dry of all available nutrients, out she popped. Along with all the other associated *matter* and a fine crop of haemorrhoids. I had naïvely thought I would look smaller once she was on the outside, but my stomach seemed to be exactly the same size only floppier.

Foolishly, I had promised an old friend to try her method of wrapping a towel round your middle as soon as the baby is born. She claimed it really was the best way back to a flat tummy. A nurse caught me at it and told me that it was tied too loosely and it wouldn't work unless it was really, really tight. Just to add to all the other discomforts I was experiencing hours after labour. Personally, I don't think it works unless you dip it first in plaster of Paris and leave it in place for at least six months. I decided after all that the tummy would hardly notice as it was being overshadowed by these two enormous jugs that tended to deflect attention from the other bits of wobbly flesh. That wasn't so bad – after all I'd always hankered after an ample bosom. Not one that leaked, though. I was reminded of a remark made to me years before by a woman who maintained that having a baby involved complete loss of personal dignity. With industrial-strength padding in all the places that used to be barely covered by wisps of lace, I could see what she meant.

(Incidentally, despite the fact that it is a rich seam of comedy, and bucking the trend somewhat, I'm not even going to talk about sex. Suffice to say that I didn't fancy it much for a while after childbirth. I knew what it could lead to.)

But time heals all wounds (if not stretch marks) and women's bodies can recover from the sort of physical drubbing which, if it happened in an accident, would have us hospitalised for a month. Maybe that's why it's called the miracle of birth: being torn apart at the seams is what is *supposed* to happen. You just sit on a rubber ring for a week then forget all about it. I call that miraculous.

By the time my daughter was a year old the physical wreck that was my body had returned to the physical wreck it was before I had her. Except I do remember wondering whether my knees always cracked like that, or whether I was just noticing it more. You do tend to spend more time close to the floor when there's a toddler around. This, incidentally, is a factor that is never taken into account when every so often some Sunday newspaper helpfully calculates how many squillions of pounds it costs to bring up a child. They never mention trousers, and yet it is well known that mothers' jeans always rip at the knees much quicker than those of childless women. Or maybe that was just peculiar to me because jeans were all I ever wore, week in week out. It was a blow when I realised that, although I could fit into my normal clothes again, there was absolutely no point in wearing them. I became a stranger to skirts, and my winter coat – bought when I was pregnant but unaware of it – was warm but useless. However icily the wind might be blowing across the park, an ankle-skimming garment was hopeless when I spent so much time squatting down in mud and piles of leaves. I always thought I wore practical, comfortable clothes, but compared to the outfits I adopted when I was looking after a toddler, I had spent the previous years decked out like a Christmas tree in heels. Drop earrings were out of the question, unless I wanted my lobes yanked into beagle ears; even necklaces and scarves became dangerous accessories. One thing I refused to compromise on, however, was my long hair – even though I did lose a few fistfuls while she was very small. My reasoning was that she had ruined everything else from the neck down and I would like to keep my head intact (fat chance). Besides which, as long as either the baby or the hair was tied up, it wasn't a problem.

But the physical changes are for the most, unless you are very unlucky, either temporary or cause for weary resignation. The change in mental outlook stays with you. It's not just the dawning appreciation of the merits of acrylic over linen. It's more fundamental than that. (Although, come to think of it, what could be more fundamental than that when you have to do your own ironing?)

The worry levels start to rise when you are pregnant. You become aware that you are living permanently at a low-level but constant pitch of anxiety. It never leaves you and doesn't improve when the baby is born. If my baby daughter didn't sleep I worried that there was something desperately wrong with her. If she decided to sleep for hours I had to check every five minutes that she wasn't dead, instead of regarding it as a well-earned opportunity to loaf about on the sofa watching *Quincy*. And it affects every area of your life. A friend, an enthusiastic theatre-goer, pre-pregnancy went to see and enjoyed *Antony and Cleopatra*. Years later, with two small daughters tucked up with the babysitter, she found herself again in a theatre watching Shakespeare's tragedy and all she could think about was

'But Cleopatra has children! What's going to happen to her children?' Great swathes of literature and art are suddenly closed to you because children, instead of being mere plot-carriers, are now the object of your deepest concerns and fears and you can't concentrate on the poetry. Think about *Madama Butterfly*. Of course it's sad, but I defy any mother watching it to stop herself from thinking not, 'What a glorious artist Puccini was,' but 'Why, instead of packing him off to relations for the weekend, did she choose to blindfold her son? And, more importantly, how did she do it? How come he didn't whine, fight, wriggle and tear it off, then kick her to a pulp in a fit of rage before she had a chance to top herself? And how could she even consider doing that to her own son?'

Poetry is lost to you, but you can find yourself reduced to a puddle of tears by the most appalling schmaltz. I sniffed so loudly during *Rugrats in Paris*, because Chuckie hasn't got a mum, that I got looks. The work of that well-known family entertainer, Walt Disney, is littered with dead and missing parents and abandoned babies. We never find out what happened to Snow White's real mum or Mowgli's parents, but *Tarzan* and *Lilo and Stitch*, for example, involve blood-thirsty leopards and fatal car crashes so that I can sob over the poor motherless mites. And let's not forget Bambi's mother. Let us never forget Bambi's mother. I'm filling up now, but all this death and mayhem doesn't seem to bother my daughter at all. I must have taught her so well to take anything on the screen with a pinch of salt that she will take it on herself to reassure me that 'It's all right, Mummy, it isn't real.'

No it isn't real, it's children's entertainment, apparently, and I can always be cheered up by the happy endings. It's the real stuff which plants that feeling of deep and abiding fear that can't be shaken. Watching the news can be seriously traumatic, and I would very much like to bite the next journalist I hear using the phrase 'every parent's nightmare'. Every health scare, freak accident or lost battle with fatal illness that I hear about hits me like a physical blow. Stories of child abuse make me want to hug my daughter so tight her ribs are in danger of breaking – which would be the cruellest form of irony. I used to take life as it came; now I have developed a marked tendency to worry about things that are not likely to happen.

Sometimes things do happen, and nursing skills are called into action. Hitherto my Florence Nightingale act had been limited to growling 'Take an aspirin and go to bed' should anybody need pandering to. I might throw in the odd Lem-Sip if pushed, but diagnostics was never my strong point. Now, instead of having to listen impatiently to someone describing every symptom in minute detail, I was faced with a small baby who definitely had something wrong with her, but I didn't know what it was. However many times I read the medical section of the childcare manual, there was always one glaring omission. It told me how to remove foreign objects from the eye and how to deal with snake bites, but there was nothing at all on how not to panic. I really wasn't used to this sense of responsibility in my life and it was a change I could have done without. But I read the medical books and leaflets from the surgery so I wouldn't be caught out by any strange or terrifying symptoms. So when I saw the red spots I was confident enough to identify it immediately as chickenpox and say to my husband 'It's OK, some children get a few spots and a raised temperature and they hardly notice it.' Thirty-six hours later at four in the morning I was sobbing over my daughter's leper-like body as I tried and failed to ease her suffering a little. I remember being vaguely sympathetic to other people's coughs and colds and unthreatening viruses before, but never had I wished to actually take somebody else's illness on myself. (I must have wished a bit too fervently, though, because I cried even harder when three weeks later I came back from work with a splitting headache and my fully recovered daughter said to me brightly 'Mummy, you're all lumpy.')

So, instead of regarding a sore throat as a great opportunity to stay at home and listen to Radio Four in my pyjamas, illness had become a cause for major concern. Every little sneeze seemed to whisper disease. This was not good. I had never had a problem with sickness before, and used to scoff at people who caught a cold and called it flu. But when she manifested any symptom at all, alarm bells would start ringing loudly. How could this have happened to me? I was of the sensible, 'fresh air and brisk walks will soon put the colour back in your cheeks' school of nursing and regarded medical encyclopaedias as hypochondriacs' handbooks. Now I can quote them. Do I want to know about all these dangers or not? Am I neglecting my respon-sibilities if I'm not aware of every tiny symptom that could herald something more serious, or would I be turning myself into a hypochondriac by proxy? Even if I do try to be sensible about risk, we all know that at three o'clock in the morning, *all* symptoms are suggestive of meningitis.

I was once told a story over the tea table that I would like to repeat here. A woman had a cold and a runny nose that just wouldn't go away. Long after all other symptoms had disappeared she was still left with a dribbling hooter. After a long time and various trips to pharmacists, doctors and Chinese herbalists for all I know, she saw a specialist who identified the dripping stuff as brain fluid that was leaking out of her nose and she was rushed to hospital for an emer-gency operation. I know you won't thank me for sharing that with you but I'm damned if I'm going to suffer alone every time my daughter gets a fit of the sniffles.

So having spent a hitherto trouble-free life which I

skipped through singing a happy song I am now resigned to the fact that I will spend the rest of my days being scared. It might be from the little bursts of adrenalin you get when children run too near the kerb, tip back on their chairs or suddenly come barrelling into the kitchen when pots are bubbling fiercely on the stove and you find yourself shouting, not with anger, but with fear. I might be scared by world events, a story of a child struck down by an incredibly rare disease or tragedy too close to home. Anything might happen and it probably won't, but nothing can stop me worrying about it. You say 'adventure playground' and I say 'accident waiting to happen'. Among the post-birth physical changes I forgot to include the ineradicable seams of anxiety imprinted on my face.

I often wondered whether this tendency to imagine freak accidents and worry constantly about unlikely misadventures was something to do with me being, how shall I say, a woman of more mature years. I was one of the growing band of women who had to endure the humiliation of having 'elderly primigravida' writ large on my hospital notes. I suspected that if I'd been allowed a closer squint at those notes they might have had 'old trout up the spout' scrawled across them as a reminder to the young whippersnapper prodding me about to prod a little more gently. But even if I was no spring chicken, I did have the advantage of being a tough old bird, and sailed through pregnancy and

birth with a lot less trouble than some teenage hypochondriacs I could mention.

But the teenagers undoubtedly got their own back when
it came to life after birth. As I prowled round the playcentre
calculating the devastating effect that one grain of sand
could have if lodged in the eye, huddles of young mothers
gossiped and smoked in the corner of the playground while
their offspring hurtled round at full throttle, throwing themselves off slides and running full-pitch into walls.
Occasionally one of the mothers would be alerted by a
familiar roaring sound and would saunter over to adminis-
ter kisses, Band-Aid, full body plaster or whatever was
required before returning to her conversation. Meanwhile,
I noticed that I wasn't alone in hovering, arms outstretched,
beside the tiny little climbing frame. I and others of a similar
age would be poised, trembling with fear, ready to catch our
tumbling toddlers, who were deliberately provoking us by
insisting on climbing on the climbing frame and sliding
down the slide. It did sometimes occur to me that I might be
being a little over-protective, and the accident most likely to
happen would be two forty-somethings colliding at great
speed as they raced round the apparatus trying to be in
place for catching duty. But didn't those young mothers see
all the dangers? Had they no imagination? Or did I have too
much? You would think that with the wisdom of age I would
be better equipped to calculate risk and be a lot more calm

and composed than a teenager faced with the responsibility of caring for a small child. But it never seemed to work like that. My experience of life had obviously just taught me how awful it can be, and although hitherto I had been able to cope with anything it could throw at me, it was different coping with life throwing things at my daughter. And her throwing them back.

So of course becoming a parent changes you. There wouldn't be much bloody point in having kids if everything stayed the same. So why do we have them? Is it an act of utter selflessness or complete selfishness? I don't care to examine my motives too closely. We'd do anything for our kids, we say, and embrace every personal sacrifice gladly, always putting them first and revelling in our selfless love and devotion. But the object of my love and care is undeniably part of me and when the flesh of my flesh does something I thoroughly disapprove of I take it as a personal affront. I want to mould her into a wonderful human being, something I can be proud of as my best work – a reflection, in other words, of my own best self. Isn't that terribly selfish?

Chapter Four

Communication breakdown

As OUR DAUGHTER GREW, SO DID OUR UNDER-standing of each other – up to a point. I can't decide which phrase has been uttered more often in this house: 'I can't wait for her to learn to talk' or 'Can't you get her to shut up for five minutes?'

I was always impressed at the interpreting skills of mothers with toddlers. I've seen it countless times: 'Aberdeen leasing! Aberdeen leasing!' the kid insists and the mother replies, 'OK. What colour do you want?' 'Rollmop.' 'There isn't one. You can have a red one.' And the child trots off happily, clutching a rollmop aberdeen leasing, apparently under the impression that she's just had a normal conver-sation. With my own prattling babe in attendance I realised it isn't a spooky mind-reading thing after all, it just comes naturally when you have to live with somebody who talks scribble. Even though my own interpreting skills became quite good with practice, there were still moments of complete perplexity. 'Bassalilly! Bassalilly!' was a mystery to me. I assumed my daughter was telling me she had an unpleasant virus and it took me quite a few minutes of linguistic detective work (opening cupboard doors and proffering various objects) before I realised she wanted spaghetti. I cracked that one, but sometimes she defeated even my considerable powers of detection and I was reduced to confessing, 'No, sorry, you've got me there.' Such admissions of failure were met with yells of frustration or, worse, the deep sigh and pitying stare at the idiot woman who couldn't understand simple instructions. I dare say when she's haranguing me with a stream of well-chosen and incisive insults I shall look back fondly to the time when the only word she could say with perfect clarity was 'fart', but at the time communication was often a rather hit and miss affair.

A friend of mine was once at her wits' end with her youngest son's inability to express what was obviously a deep-felt need. Opting for the proffering method, she had nearly emptied her kitchen cupboards before the truth dawned. Number-one son, in an act of sheer childish cruelty, had sent his barely-speaking brother to ask for hundreds and thousands. Could have marked the poor little blighter for life, but what do older brothers care?

In between the bawling and puking stage and the development into a running commentator on all aspects of life, our daughter's acquisition of speech was not always the unalloyed joy we assumed it would be. The process was sometimes hilarious, often completely baffling and occasionally vaguely troubling. The ability to talk, she soon found out, is the perfect opportunity to start giving peremptory orders. Sometimes she betrayed a worrying resemblance to Father Jack: 'Drink!' Apart from that, the things she chose to vocalise followed no logical thought processes as far as I could see. God knows I'm always banging on about truth and beauty, so why, from the rich treasure of the English language, did she choose to say 'hoover'? It's not as if we talk about it, or even use it much. Odd, until I decided that this too came under the category of peremptory orders, and that when she said 'hoover' it was merely shorthand for 'Get this place cleaned up, woman, I've just had a biscuit.'

The opportunities for misunderstanding are of French farce proportions. Have you noticed that whenever a child hands something over, an adult will *invariably* say 'Is that for me?' So, when pressing a half-chewed chocolate or dead snail into my hand my daughter always intoned solemnly 'For me.' The grammar needed work, but I couldn't fault her logic. Having spent hours drilling into her the importance of avoiding anything hot, I once remarked gaily as I whipped her pyjamas off the radiator, 'Lovely jimjams, wear 'em while they're hot,' only to be met with deep hostility and a point-blank refusal to put them on. We added 'warm' to the vocabulary soon afterwards, and did some extra work on 'drollery', 'jest' and 'bon mot'.

And then there's the swearing. I admit that ours is not the sort of household where never is heard a discouraging word. My language can sometimes be a mite colourful, and that colour tends to be blue. So unless I could change the habits of a lifetime I knew that sooner or later she was going to come out with something I'd rather she hadn't. I tried to prepare my sternly disapproving face in readiness, but in the event it was never used. Why? Because a toddler saying gravely 'Oh bugger' is terribly funny, and it's not easy trying to explain that it's not acceptable behaviour when guffawing uncontrollably. Admittedly, I might not have been so amused by 'Oh, fucking hell' but there's something intensely comical about 'bugger'. Sorry if that's another admission of bad motherhood.

I also learned from the experience of a French friend who was mortified by her young daughter burbling away merrily 'Fok, fok, fok,' and felt obliged to explain, 'Phoque, phoque, she's saying phoque – it's French for seal... She has a toy seal, furry thing, sweet, big eyes ...' When she found herself telling complete strangers at bus stops that her daughter was not a foul-mouthed little madam, but merely

French, she suddenly thought 'Oh, phoque this,' and adopted the English maxim, 'Never apologise, never explain.' She was a lot calmer after that.

Having two languages to choose from can have its advantages, though. When my own little madam came out with some completely incomprehensible bilge, I could lie blatantly and maintain that she was in fact speaking perfect Czech – her father's native tongue. A harmless stratagem, but only a short-term one. As her speech became clearer even I would be hard put to claim, straight-faced, that 'Christonabike' is a legitimate Czech word. Never mind, I thought, I'll blame the school. Naturally, in her heated avowal that she was only saying what Mummy said when she dropped a plate, her diction and vocabulary were perfect.

Having another language in the mixture certainly added a certain piquancy to the whole business of learning to talk. It does make things interesting, such as the time she remarked innocently when watching a video 'I didn't know Tarzan was Czech.' She obviously hadn't noticed that Snow White, Dumbo and the Iron Giant were also fluent Czech speakers, each of the seven dwarves had been renamed and Eldorado has been transplanted to Bohemia. (Actually, not Dumbo, but certainly the rest of the cast.) It can add a little confusion as well.

'What are you eating?' a friend asked her once.

'Parky.'

'What?'

(Slightly louder) 'Parky'

'I said what are you eating?'

(With an air of complete exasperation) 'PARKY!'

It simply didn't occur to her that her friend didn't know what parky were. That was what they were always called and surely everyone knew that. (They're frankfurters, if you're interested.) Between our daughter mangling the language and her Spanish best friend Dolores I'm surprised either of them managed to learn any English at all, but their use of words gave an insight into the workings of the child brain. When Dolores had become more fluent in English she announced one day:

'Did you know a fairy is dead?'

'A fairy?'

'Oh, no, not a fairy, a princess.'

After a moment of contemplation I ventured
    cautiously: 'Do you mean the Queen Mother?'

'Yeah, yeah, that's it.'

There was a certain mad logic in that conversation, but I wasn't so sure about the following exchange with our daughter. We were ruthlessly drilling her in vocabulary and pretending it was a game.

'What's the English for... jezevec?'

'Badger!'

'Králík?'

'Rabbit!'

'Klokan?'

'Kangaroo!' (Are you detecting a theme here?)

'Morče?'

'Bacon!'

'Bacon? *Bacon?*'

'Morče' is in fact the Czech word for guinea pig, so I suppose there was some sort of tenuous connection with rashers, but God knows what was going on in the language section of her brain at that moment. Misfiring on all cylinders, I suspect.

In the early stages (and I hope other parents do this too) instead of correcting and refining our daughter's use of English, we just took on her linguistic fantasias and incorporated them into our own speech. I suppose it's OK within the confines of your own home to start talking about aminals and bindons (big ones) but half the time we didn't realise we were doing it. When she was very young she developed a habit of bleating like a goat whenever she heard a loud noise. We'd heard it so often we started doing it ourselves. Fine, until the day when my husband was sitting in a café with a friend and somebody dropped a tray of cutlery. He only paused for a second in his fascinating narrative to say 'Meeeh' before carrying on – hardly missing a beat. The oddest thing about it was not that he'd done it, but that his friend didn't comment at all. Did he think that animal noises were a normal part of conversation? Did he not like to mention it for fear of opening a vein of deep psychosis? Of course, by the time my husband realised what he'd done it was too late to explain – and two seconds is too long in that sort of situation – so he ignored it as well and just carried on. He came home bursting with glee but a little embarrassed as well. The sooner she learned to talk properly the better, before we all reverted to grunts and barks in our efforts to communicate.

Beyond the stage of trying to work out what 'bassalilly' meant we progressed to 'conversations', where she learned to use the language to her own advantage.

'Mummy, look, it's bleeding!'

'It's fine, I can't see any blood.'

'That's because it's *dry* bleeding!'

Oh, terrific. It's not enough to take out shares in Elastoplast, I now have to tend to non-existent wounds as well. My desire for her to be inventive with the language waned a little after she'd come up with that particular concept.

This sort of stuff (which all comes into the category of 'Golly! The things they say!') kept us amused, but after a while we established the difference between sniggering behind our hands when she got something hilariously wrong and actually sharing a joke. Her first attempts at a genuine jest usually involved the juxtaposition of opposites: 'The window's broken. Hooray! Hooray! I've spilt my drink. Hooray! Hooray!' and so on and so on for however long the car journey or our patience lasted. She pretty soon added spoonerisms to slapstick as her favourite forms of humour: 'You said "lut the pight on!" Ha ha ha!' And any sort of linguistic mistake, such as calling her teacher by the cat's name, is absolutely killing. She has recently discovered the computer, and one of her favourite pastimes is 'typing'. This involves me reading out *Rapunzel* word by word (or letter by letter for the difficult ones) while she laboriously taps it all out on the keyboard. I can't tell you what fun this is for me, and I was once about to down tools and open a bottle when I glanced at the screen and saw she had typed 'A few months later she gave birth to a beautiful baby girk.' (The preceding sentence did *not* involve rampant sexual activity, in case you're wondering.) We got an awful lot of mileage out of that one. Singing 'I enjoy being a girk'; 'Girks and boys come out to play'; 'What are little girks made of?' and so on took us all through bathtime and up to bedtime. Simple, harmless fun, but it reminded me how far she had travelled beyond goat bleats.

The discovery of a sense of humour, however puerile (which, to be honest, suits me just fine) was probably the most important part of acquiring language, and the most deeply satisfying. If I make a joke I want somebody to laugh, and the fact that she can now occasionally appreciate my little sallies has made a big difference to our relationship. (Although it will still be a while before I try her out on my own favourite joke: 'What are you having for dinner?' 'Chicken Tarka.' 'What's that?' 'It's like chicken tikka only otter.' For now we'll keep it simple and infantile. Girks and burps are about our level.) I notice, however, that if she can roll around on the floor at some idiocy of Mummy's, it's not so funny when the humour is directed against her. She can dish it out but she can't take it. 'Can I have a lemon?' 'You can have a lemon to suck by all means but I think you mean melon.' 'That's what I said!' Defensiveness and blatant lying we still have to work on.

Along the way of honing our communication skills there was something else that required a little application. Once she got past the stage of calling 'upstairs' 'uppities' and could string a sentence together it dawned on us that she was spending a lot of time in a playground ringing with more glottal stops than Saudi Arabia. Not to put too fine a point on it, I was determined that the letter T should figure quite prominently in her speech, as it didn't seem to exist in the street. Call me old-fashioned, but I didn't want her ending up as a children's TV presenter – or worse, with the sort of ridiculous man-of-the-people accent that Tony Blair affects. What is that all about? Anyway, constant correction and drilling was the only answer. I had turned into my father, of course, who used to fulminate loudly against the horrors of the London accent. In vain I would argue that it was only a regional variation, and exactly the same as being brought up in Devon and having a rich country burr: we dropped our Hs at our peril. So I'm afraid she got exactly the same treatment as I did – and so did some of her friends. I once came into the kitchen when my husband was haranguing the now eloquent Dolores: 'It's *water*! Not waw-ah. If you want some water I'll get you some, but we haven't got any waw-ah because there's no such thing!' The bizarre nature of a Czech berating a Spaniard on the pronunciation of English wasn't lost on me, and I bet there's a very bemused English teacher in Madrid right now, trying to make sense of a little girl whose English is fluent but probably incomprehensible outside the Thames valley.

Having 'mastered' speaking and progressed from drooling bleater to witty sophisticate, next there was the business of getting it all down on paper. Compared with the rest of Europe, I thought, maybe children in this country were forced into reading and writing at a rather young age, but they seemed to enjoy it, and I was surprised at her rapid grasp of letters. I mentioned this to her teacher, who told me: 'Well, a lot of people say that, and really we can't claim any credit for it. It seems like suddenly something clicks and they're off.' He was perfectly right. Suddenly she was off, and in much the same way as when she got the hang of talking, once she started she couldn't stop. Bus tickets, posters, cornflake packets, traffic signs, the occasional book – all were laboriously spelt out. Even number plates, which, owing to the Czechs' rather cavalier attitude to vowels, often spell proper words, whether she recognises them as such or not. 'KRK' (neck) is a favourite, regularly parked by the school, but any combination of letters will be pronounced out loud, much to the consternation of her father one morning. Skipping along on her merry way to school she suddenly proclaimed in perfect Czech:

'FUCK.'

'What?'

'There, over there on the red car: MRD.'

She was right, it did say 'mrd' which also happens to be Czech for 'fuck'. I swear she didn't know that, but it gave her dad a bit of a bad moment.

But when she couldn't read things for herself, she was still anxious to know what they meant, so would spell things out helpfully for Mummy to translate. I've spent many happy hours loitering outside the downstairs toilet (which also houses the washing machine) while she shouts through the door. It helps to have a mental picture of what's inside the toilet during these sessions, as it speeds things up a bit.

'What does P-E-R-S-I-L spell?'

'Persil.'

'What about N-O-N-B-I-O…'

'Non biological.'

'Z…'

'Zanussi. Haven't you finished yet?'

There is also a 'stylish and practical' shelving arrange-ment along the back wall of the smallest room (offcuts of wood propped up on paperbacks). This was the explanation for the joyous shout of 'D. M. Thomas!' which came through the door. Yes, well, I think we'll keep that one propping up the shelves for a while in case your reading is better than I think it is.

And with reading comes writing. Any parent's heart overflows at the sight of those first wobbly letters, and I pretty soon made sure she knew how to write 'I love you mummy' – just to make me feel good. She wasn't going to stop at meaningless phrases though, and left to her own devices would scribble away at 'stories' and 'letters'. Goodness knows what a neighbour thought when she received a missive through her letterbox explaining that two Polish men had come to put a new fence up and there were loads of snails. I trust she was fascinated, once she managed to decipher it. Knowing my daughter's aptitude for imparting useless information I smiled in anticipation when she came back from a YMCA holiday club waving a piece of paper and trilling excitedly 'Look! I made this for you!' I was a bit taken aback when I opened it up. Not at the picture of myself (my hair never looks that messy, even first thing in the morning) but at what she had scrawled underneath: 'Dear mummy I love you bat not wene you shawt at me.' I was mortified. Dolores's mum had taken them both to the club and picked them up, so I hadn't even been there on that day. What were those youth workers going to think? This poor little girl had some hard-bitten career woman as a mother who couldn't be bothered to look after her own daughter except to shout at her! Never mind, I thought, perhaps they felt sorry for her and gave her special treatment. Then I started getting a bit shirty at the injustice of it. 'What do you mean, shout at you? I never shout at you. I might raise my voice occasionally but that's perfectly acceptable. Good grief, you don't know what shouting is! You can hear Sharon's mother half a bloody mile away. *That's* shouting!' I realised that my voice had indeed risen slightly, so backtracked wildly. 'It's lovely. Thank you very much.' Even so, I was still a bit miffed. It was bad enough having to deal with those occasions when their loud remarks can cause embarrassment (if not fisticuffs) without them writing it all down as hard evidence.

But if I was secretly proud of her fantastic literary skills, I was soon brought heavily down to earth. On a long car journey we indulged her in a game of I Spy. I wanted to show off to her grandmother and aunt just how clever she was – she can even spell Konopicky, after all, which is more than a lot of people can. We were doing quite well, when she came up with 'I spy with my little eye, something beginning with CH.'

There were four other people in that car, and we went through everything we could think of, let alone see. Scraping the bottom of the barrel, 'cheerful child', 'chirpy bird', 'Chumba-Wumba' and 'cheerleader' were all triumphantly rejected as we made wilder and wilder guesses. Eventually we all admitted defeat and she announced with a flourish that the word each of us numskulls had failed to get was 'traffic'. Obviously my skills at elocution training (or chraining) were sadly lacking. Oh well, at least she puts a T in the middle of words, if not at the beginning.

But it's wonderful having someone around who I can actually talk to, although she remains distinctly uncommunicative in certain areas. 'What was it like at school today?' gets the invariable reply: 'OK.' 'But what did you *do*?' [Deep sigh] 'Oh, it was just work, work, work.' Forgive me for being a little sceptical about the slave-driving that goes on in Key

Stage 1, but perhaps she's right not to talk about it too much. Having heard her parents droning on endlessly about the minutiae of office politics she's probably decided that it's a bit tedious, and she may have a point. She's more forthcoming when something really interesting happens, such as when David broke his arm 'in two places – and he had chickenpox!' Poor David was an object of real interest for a while, but I'm damned if I can get out of her what all this 'work, work, work' constitutes. But at least I'm confident that when she does choose to divulge information, it's usually pretty accurate. She hasn't reached the stage of dissimulating, hiding things or trying to pull the wool over my eyes (saving it up for the teenage years, no doubt) and we have learned to listen to what she says. I made some remark once about a local child being out with her grandfather and was immediately corrected: 'That's her dad.' Surely not, we scoffed, *that's* her dad, the much younger man. 'No, that's her uncle.' She was quite adamant, but we just ignored her – that man was far too old to be Jenny's father, she'd just got it wrong and we were right. Were we hell. Relying on the word of a five-year-old might seem like dodgy ground, but after all, these were her friends and in her social circle she was far more likely to have got the proper low-down on family structures. Perhaps Jenny's dad wasn't as old as he looked – quite probably the strain of having a small daughter had aged him prematurely, my husband argued, not without feeling. We should learn to trust her word, although when she told me there was a new girl in her class called Cinderella, I felt I really ought to check that she'd got the name right.

'Cinderella? Are you sure?'

'Yes. She's called Cinderella. Our teacher told us.'

'Oh. Fine. [pause and snigger] Has she got any sisters?'

She was right again, although I never really got to know Cinderella properly because, strangely, she only stayed at the school for as long as the circus was in town.

Now, when our daughter talks, we listen. It's a good arrangement (although not one that always works in reverse, I note) and, barring the occasional sulks and the odd (very odd) misunderstandings, we communicate with each other freely and at great length. But in the field of communication there are still some things she has to learn. After three years as her bosom buddy, Dolores has been sorely missed since she moved back to Spain. Even so I have as yet neglected to tell my daughter how the email works. She'll just have to shout louder so she can be heard in Madrid. She probably could, too.

Chapter Five

Oh, what is it now?

I T WAS FIVE O'CLOCK ON A WARM SUNNY AFTER-
noon and I was returning from work – a full hour
before my usual time. Getting home early from work always
used to be a rare treat, and in theory I would be getting a
whole extra hour of my daughter's company, but as I
approached my house I imagined the scene that would
greet me. Kids all over the playground and the street,
possibly spilling into my house as well. The au pair draped
over the roundabout, coated in full slap and trying to look
alluring for the benefit of the local toughs. Noise, demands,
irritations.

I went into a pub. A very pleasant, newly refurbished
pub about ten minutes' walk from my house that had been
there for at least three years and I had never before set foot

in. I sat for an hour with a large (and shockingly expensive) glass of wine, pretending to be going over some notes but in reality just not going home. I arrived there eventually at my usual time and hoped the au pair wouldn't smell alcohol on my breath.

Naturally I felt so guilty about my truancy I told everyone about it. I was faintly surprised and vastly relieved that, far from being shocked that I had abandoned my post so irresponsibly, quite a few people admitted to the same reluctance to rush to the bosom of the family when the working day was over. One man would regularly park his car at the end of his street and sit there in silence and isolation for at least half an hour before feeling strong enough to plunge into the domestic bliss of his household. Sitting in the car out of reach of your home turned out to be quite a popular form of parental relaxation. Sitting in the pub was just a variation on a theme, and chosen principally because I can't drive, but even I have enjoyed the confines of the car on occasions. 'Oh, no,' I'd say. 'Don't disturb her, just bring me a book and I'll sit with her until she wakes up.' Brilliant. The perfect excuse not to have to *do* anything.

Having settled into the routine of motherhood, the novelty had long since worn off and it was now just an accepted part of living. With the routine, however, came the desire for the occasional escape from my loved ones, which turned out to be stronger than I had originally thought it would be. Among the myriad things that they don't tell you, and even if they did, you couldn't quite grasp until you were experiencing it yourself, is that childcare can be really *really* irritating. And when it's not irritating it's boring.

Children really make you ride that rollercoaster of emotions from the overwhelming joy of new parenthood to the apoplectic rage at some unspeakable behaviour that they've been warned about a thousand times already. In between the rollercoaster highs and lows, however, is the scenic railway of day-to-day parenting – or, more accurately, the Virgin Rail. Gets there in the end but is deeply annoying on the way. I'm not talking about the sort of disobedience that cries out for professional help, or the bowel-clenching brushes with danger that kids indulge in on a whim, just to keep us on our toes. It's the relentless contrariness of children. Nothing in isolation that would justify parental wrath, but cumulatively the drip, drip, drip of constant vex-ations is enough to send you into a corner with your head in your hands, rocking to and fro and moaning softly. That's why we hide in cars or sit on park benches in the rain. We're just enjoying the absence of demands.

Babies are incapable of being deliberately naughty, but by God they certainly know how to needle you. I don't know why my daughter had to leave a constant trail of shoes and socks from house to high street – just in case I couldn't find my way back there I suppose – and I don't know why her favourite toy was my face. Having to smile while having my bottom lip yanked sideways was just one of the tests of maternal love I had to pass. Helpless as they are, babies still find a thousand ways of exercising their tiny power. Being woken three times a night is too knackering to be classed as merely irksome, but when a baby decides to take a lavish dump every time you put a clean nappy on her it's enough to make anybody's lips twitch. After about the seventeenth time I was pretty well convinced that she was doing it on purpose. That look of bemused wonderment on her face didn't fool me a bit. One of my favourite bedtime croonings was 'Speak roughly to your little girl and beat her when she sneezes/ She only does it to annoy because she knows it teases.' It made me feel better, anyway. I knew that I was tired and therefore more prone to general tetchiness and it wasn't her fault, but it didn't stop me from being snappy. It's terribly unfair to get hacked off with a baby, but at least it got her used at a young age to seeing Mummy grinding her teeth or leaving the room very suddenly, because the vex factor wasn't going to get any less as she got older.

From the first moment of breast-feeding that carried on for the next two hours, I realised that I was no longer in control of my own physical movement. I'm ashamed to say that she earned the name of 'Strugglebugger' during the period before walking but while she was discovering the strength in her limbs. Carrying her around was like wrestling an octopus as she strained and heaved and tried to use me as a springboard. But then she pretty soon found that she was perfectly able to walk as long as she held on some part of Mummy at the same time, whatever position Mummy happened to be in when she decided to launch herself off. Such fun, those impromptu games of Twister while I tried to rearrange my limbs into suitable supports and answer the phone at the same time. But it was just a passing phase. When she mastered walking she was able to do that cute thing that toddlers do of handing you things that are just out of reach then walking briskly away, so you either fall over yourself in an attempt to catch whatever it is, or drop it on the floor. Butter side down, usually. Putting her coat on invariably turned into a matador dance as I tried to put her right sleeve on while she parried with her left. Turning my back for a second to collect my own coat would give her just enough time to take her shoes off. Again. And although I was overjoyed when she showed some evidence of being able to count, my joy was tempered somewhat by the fact that she couldn't put this new skill to any use. Like counting how many hands I have. Coming down the stairs with armfuls of washing and a bunch of unanswered letters between my teeth was always her cue to say 'Mummy, hold on this.' And even at her advanced stage of life she still has what I call 'Threshold Syndrome'. Always anxious to be the first out of the door she then stops immediately on the doorstep, sniffing the air like a cat, while the rest of us pile up behind her like the elephants in *The Jungle Book*. If I ever cross the threshold, however, i.e., leave the room in which she is situated, I can't take two steps without being called back on some urgent business. Words have been exchanged on this subject on more than one occasion. 'If you want me, why can't you come and get me? Why do I always have to go running after you?' I can't remember her answer, probably because she has no valid excuse for such unforgivable behaviour.

And if I am required to drop everything at every querulous request for attention, I note with displeasure that the same is not true for her. Her sense of urgency evaporates as soon as some urgency really is required.

'Can you *please* put your shoes on and get your schoolbag!'

'I've just got to finish this drawing.'

'You don't have to finish it *now*, we're going to be late!'

(After a few more minutes of essential and elaborate colouring in) 'Let me see, which shoes shall I wear?'

'*The blue ones!* Just put them on – look at the time!'

'I haven't said goodbye to Rex.'

'Forget the cat, just hurry up!'

'I don't like this jumper, can I wear the other one?'

'Good God do you not know the *meaning* of the
   word procrastinate?'

'No.'

'Well you're doing it now! *Just get out of the door!*'

Why, in the name of everything sacred, do children have no
sense of timing at all?

Oh well, needling Mummy into a frenzy is all good fun.
And on the subject of fun, I do think that stimulating play is
very important for children. Other sorts of stimulants can be
very important for their parents, too, after a particularly
creative session with the paintbrush. One man I know
admitted that he eventually refused to do any more painting
with his small daughter because he found the whole experience just too maddening, and I was reminded of that happy
afternoon when my daughter painted her arms red. It was
only recently that I heard a mother saying that her son was
delighted with the model he'd made at school 'because he's
not allowed to do that at home' and the truth hit me like a
thunderbolt. Of course! What a fool I'd been! Just because
the Early Learning Centre sells paints it didn't mean I had to
buy them. Glue and glitter are for the playcentre, not for the

carpet in the spare room (or 'the making room' as she has chillingly renamed it). Too bloody late now, of course, as she has had years of cutting, sticking, sprinkling and smearing just because I was idiot enough to think it was good for her. It probably is, but I could have saved myself a lot of heartache and clothes if I'd only let her do it outside the house.

And those ridiculous 'craft aprons' that we are encouraged to buy just don't work. Total nudity might be preferable, but that probably wouldn't work either unless you could find a way of getting a small painted child to hover to the bathtub without touching any surfaces. During the course of our daughter's artistic career she had a brief but worrying period when her favourite paint colour was black. I'd done all the right things. We were outside in the garden, she was wearing old clothes and an apron and I was keeping well away from the spatters. I managed to get the apron off her at arm's length and hang it on the washing line, meaning to hose it down later. A gust of wind caught it and it plastered itself all over my shirt. I very much wanted to scream at that point but managed to keep my voice down to a sort of Marge Simpson hurumph. It wasn't the only time I was tempted to throw all the paints in the bin. At least she's grown out of finger painting. It still makes me shudder to think of it.

But even if I made a major error with the arts and crafts

lark, other things like cooking and gardening in which I like to encourage an interest have to be done at home. Well, no, strictly speaking they don't *have* to be done at home, but to sign her up for the RHS and a Cordon Bleu course would be taking things a little far, even for the sake of my sanity. So I dutifully taught her to dig holes and sprinkle seeds, wave a wooden spoon about and drop butter on the floor, but the temptation to snatch things out of her hands and do it myself was sometimes very, very strong. Re-seeding the lawn was fun, and the grass did grow, but only where the seeds had been carefully sprinkled all over the flowerbeds. When the neighbours could hear me yelling 'Just the *brown* ones!' I hope they guessed I was teaching her how to dead-head. Never mind, broken plants will grow back, and the kitchen needed cleaning anyway before two pounds of flour was thrown all over it. But those sessions with the mixing bowl did engender in her a deep interest in cookery. As evidenced by the fascinating five minutes we once spent with her ferreting through the fridge trying to find something she could bash with the steak hammer. 'This?' 'No.' 'This?' 'No.' 'This?' 'NO!'

Again, it was my bad temper that was the problem, not her capacity to be deliberately provoking. How else was she supposed to learn how to do things, except by doing them badly at first until she got the hang of it? Children want to do things themselves and I soon learned not to do anything dangerous or difficult within her sight if I didn't want her sticking her oar in. I think it's worked to a certain extent. She was actually very good at helping me paint the fence blue the other week. Except the next day I glanced into the garden and thought 'It's a bit early for the ceanothus to be blooming. Oh.' In my serene, non-irritable frame of mind I was able to half close my eyes and imagine I had a garden full of blue flowers, not a border liberally decorated with paint splashes.

But that was on a relaxed Sunday morning when I was feeling at peace with the world (we had got the fence painted, after all). At other times I'm far less patient. When engaged in any sort of domestic activity, I can't decide which phrase is the more chilling: 'I'll help you, Mummy' or 'I've got an idea.' Even worse, perhaps, is 'Shall I do that for you?' It should be a phrase to engender joy and gratitude, but not when uttered by a five-year-old and not when I'm shaving my legs. If I can just stop myself from snarling 'No, leave it alone, I'll do it myself' I may manage to groom her into a useful domestic slave, but I'm going to have to close my eyes in the meantime to all the dead plants, washing dropped in the mud, interesting flower arrangements, broken eggs and jam on the ceiling.

But even when they are sitting down quietly not doing much at all, children can still find ways to provoke you. The 'Why?' stage nearly drove me to distraction. My daughter found it vastly amusing to counter every reasoned reply with another 'Why?' until I was reduced to the state of a gibbering idiot. Every parent must have had similar 'conversations':

'Why are you doing that?'

'I want to get it finished before our visitors arrive.'

'Why?'

'Because I don't want to be washing up when they get here.'

'Why?'

'Because I'll want to talk to them.'

'Why?'

'Well, that's what you do with visitors.'

'Why?'

'Look, I didn't ask them round so they could watch me do the washing up.'

'Why?'

'Why what?'

'Why are you doing that?'

And so on and so on. To this day I don't know whether she just grew out of it or if she realised that she had pushed me to the limit and had better stop this amusing game before things started getting ugly. I knew it was another phase and I really *did* try to answer her properly but I desperately wanted to scream at her 'For God's sake just shut up!' Perhaps she sensed this, which is probably just as bad as actually yelling at her. So there I go being a bad mother again, but if I had recordings of just some of those maddening exchanges no jury would convict me.

I always maintained that children would be a lot less trying if they had a basic grasp of physics, so they didn't put long straws in short cups and wonder how the juice appeared magically on the carpet, or splash water all over the place and then complain that the bucket was empty. When faced with some questions, however, I began to wish that I'd paid a little more attention during lessons. The nature of her questioning has become more considered but the questions are sometimes equally unanswerable. 'How come you can see so much if your eyes are so small?' That's quite a good question, but one that requires a certain knowledge, which I don't have, about light refraction and the nature of lenses. Sometimes I have to give up and admit that I don't know whether ants sleep and had never given it much thought until she brought the subject up. It's deeply satisfying when I *can* explain simply some natural phenomenon, but questions like 'How does television work?' reveal the huge gaps in my knowledge of the world. I'm sure I must have known once how thunder happens, but putting it into words now involves a lot of mumbling and glossing over of basic facts. I draw the line at talking about God moving his furniture about or rumbling cloud tummies, but I know I have been forced to fall back on the old standby of 'You'd better ask your father' when I was really at my wits' end.

Those early years were a real test of my character. The flashes of anger which I was always so ashamed of afterwards were often interspersed with periods of intense boredom. The relentless routines of childcare came home to me once when I found myself kneeling on the floor thinking, 'God, I never want to change another nappy for as long as I live. I just want somebody else to do it.' But there was nobody else there to do it, and unlike cleaning out the kitchen cupboards, it's not something that can be put off for another day. In theory it should be fun playing with a two-year-old, but once you've grasped the first rule of parenthood (when attempting to entertain a small child, never do anything you're not prepared to do again 57 times in quick succession) it can get a little tedious playing 'catch' with someone who can't. Sandpits have a strictly limited attraction for me, but not for my daughter when she was small, so after I had introduced her to the concepts of digging, building, patting and smoothing (and NOT throwing) there was little for me to do except sit trickling sand through my fingers, keeping a watchful eye while thinking about all the other things I could be doing. Surely there would be something wrong with me if I *enjoyed* spending my days doing all the sorts of things that a toddler likes doing?

We still haven't quite got our literary tastes in synch, either. I drank in all the instructions to read to your child as often as possible, but it was sometimes a struggle, simply because reading her favourites over and over again sort of lost the surprise factor. And doing animal noises with a heavy cold just isn't much fun – more authentic, but not fun. Plus the fact that some of her favourites were decidedly not mine. I freely confess that I hate the Mister Men. If Roger Hargreaves wasn't already dead I might be tempted to kill him. (Although I notice that death hasn't slowed his prolific output and there are *still* new ones coming out. The fact that this didn't happen with Dickens might suggest something about the literary quality of the Mister Men books.) But she loved them so I bought them and read them and tried not to do it at breakneck speed just to get it over with. The bumper book of fairy stories was also a bit of a strain (on the wrists as well as the brain), so in order to liven things up a little for myself I took to trying out some literary criticism, which probably confused her utterly. I got quite cross about the Princess and the Frog, because she was really horrible to that poor little animal. A selfish and vile Princess gets to marry a rich and influential Prince in the end – there's no justice in that! (Although, if we're talking about art imitating life, which we won't...) Hooray for Dr

Seuss, which we both enjoy, although I would advise not having a drink before attempting *Fox in Socks*. Reading has, admittedly, got a lot more fun as my daughter has got older and we're striking out in all sorts of new directions now, but my heart used to sink at bedtime when she selected certain slim volumes for me to plough through. 'Really? You're sure you want this one *again*?' Of course she was sure. Mr bloody Tickle was a hoot.

Another confession I have to make is that I never really enjoyed bathtime as much as I was supposed to. Sometimes it was genuinely funny, but most of the time it was just something that had to be done, and squatting by a bath trying to be inventive with bubbles and toys got to be a little monotonous for me. Of course, my daughter knew she had my full attention when she was in the bath, so I was dragooned into making up little plays with assorted plastic animals, singing songs and playing games until she was getting positively wrinkly. Bathtime was fun for her, mind-numbingly dull for me – until that memorable day when the cat fell in. I know, I know, but we both laughed ourselves silly. It was one of those moments that makes it all worth while. My daughter still talks about it. The cat maintains a dignified silence on the subject.

However, the entertaining cat wasn't around when she was a toddler and I was conscious of my own boredom, and of the fact that when you are bored you are in danger of becoming boring. If your whole life revolves around child-care, which mine did for three and a half years, you can very easily find yourself not only out of the loop, but also getting a bit loopy. I didn't have much to talk about except children and it was beginning to show. A friend of mine with three small children at home understood completely. She related how she greeted her husband when he came home from work with the cheery words: 'I managed to wash all the flannels today.' Her immediate horror at her own inanity bordering on insanity made her decide she must take herself in hand. Having clean flannels is A Good Thing. Regarding it as the major achievement of your day probably isn't.

After a long time with not much to do except housework and childcare I came to the conclusion that we aren't meant to be alone with small children all day long. We're probably supposed to live in colonies like chimps, and have other adults around all the time to stop the baby from falling in the fire. However, if the alternative to my irritable and bored state of mind was to live in a commune I decided that I would rather have my nervous breakdown in private, thank you very much. There was another solution. It was time to get back to some paid employment. Naturally my daughter kicked up a little bit of fuss about me leaving the house without her for the siren call of a part-time job, but was slightly mollified when I pointed out that what it really meant was that Mummy was going to be far less cross, far less often.

Not being constantly placid, patient and smiling was something else I had to work through and accept. Something else I had to convince myself not to feel guilty about. I told myself that Pollyanna is in fact deeply irritating and probably mentally defective, and that everybody gets a little moody and fractious sometimes, even without good reason. The plain truth is that children have no need to groom themselves into interesting and amusing companions. That's not their job. Their job is to be provoking and tedious at the same time and it's our job to put up with it and teach them to get through it. Think of them as kittens, I told myself: it's not all cleaning up sick and emptying out the litter tray, there are some genuine moments of fun as well. Especially if there's a bath involved.

Chapter Six

Get a life!

I WAS ALWAYS INTERESTED BY THE CONCEPT I'D heard about of 'reinventing yourself'. More often than not it was merely journalistic shorthand for some pop singer getting a new hair colour, but it was interesting to ponder. Changing myself, my habits, the persona I presented to the world. It seemed like a nice idea until, instead of doing it myself, I had it done to me.

I had been redefined. I was first a parent and any other image of myself as fun-loving sophisticate, intellectual or flirt had to be subsumed under my primary role as cleaner-up of sick. And I'd barely even noticed. Brand new parents can be forgiven for having only one topic of conversation, but friends won't indulge you forever and sooner or later you must lift your eyes from the nappy bucket and realise that the world has been going on regardless. There is life beyond childcare, but I had made yet another fundamental error and put my life on hold when it wasn't really necessary. Although I had made a conscious decision to stay at home in the early years, after a while it did begin to get to me a little. If there was one thing worse than being bored, it was being broke and bored. Money is a great thing for getting you out of a rut, and splashing some cash around usually cheers me up no end. But I wasn't earning enough to do any dripping, let alone splashing, so I was confined to doing things that didn't cost anything. A trip to the park is lovely. Three hundred trips to the park are tedious. Of course there was a solution, but it took me a while to recognise something that was staring me in the face.

It never occurred to me that I wasn't doing all the right things. I was tired, I had no money and I was totally in love with my baby. What use had I for night life when I had my own night life of breast-feeding and the World Service to enjoy? My daughter was the biggest thing that had ever happened to me and I was so wrapped up in her world that the rest of the globe could go hang and I wouldn't miss it. We did have the odd social outing, always the three of us together and always during the day so that we would be safely home in time for her bedtime. We didn't have any relations or close friends nearby, I didn't trust anyone else with the care of my child and so somehow she reached the age of three without ever having had a babysitter. One of us was always there to put her to bed, so when eventually we did go out together for a very special occasion it was a major trauma. I felt like Madeline Kahn in *Young Frankenstein* as I murmured: 'Please don't cry, darling, you're going to get snot on my party frock. No, I can't kiss you goodbye, I've just put lipstick on.' I exaggerate my heartlessness, but it was touch and go whether we would make good our escape from our much-loved, but seriously pissed-off daughter.

Slow on the uptake as usual, it took me ages to realise that other people didn't live like this. With the gradual accumulation of chance remarks by other parents it finally dawned on me that other mothers had a bit of time off occasionally. They turned the baby over to its grandparents (not an option for me) and went to the hairdresser, or out to lunch or away for a weekend. They had babysitters. They didn't feel the need to do it all themselves. I overheard someone at nursery saying to her son 'Come on, get a move on because Mummy's going out tonight' and he didn't scream or cry or demand to talk to the NSPCC. He just got a move on. He was used to her going out sometimes. I could do that! It was a revelation. Of course, I'd made it much more difficult for myself: having spent years in the sole care of one or other of her parents, it took another couple of years to convince my daughter that babysitters were quite a normal part of life. There were tears and sulks and tantrums (and she wasn't too happy, either) but now she's fine about it, probably because it still doesn't happen very often. But it was another lesson to me. I had been quite proud that I had never left my daughter in the care of 'strangers' and was shocked to hear a working mother say that she hadn't been home in time to put her toddler to bed for over a year. In fact, far from being the perfect mother who devoted herself to her child, the way I had arranged matters was rather stupid. It wasn't good for either of us. I became more and more reluctant to leave her, so I didn't have any sort of social life beyond the telephone, and she assumed that I would always be there and became more and more difficult to leave with anyone else because she would play up something shocking. When a visitor asked me if it was safe to walk back from the tube station late at night I had to admit that I had no idea because I had never done it. I knew something had to be done but it's the sort of error that can't be corrected overnight. When we do go out now, we invariably return to find our daughter asleep on the sofa with her teeth unbrushed because she has insisted on trying to wait up for us, but at least we can go out if we want to without any seriously major tantrums. When I ran into a colleague who had just come back to work after her first maternity leave I immediately broke my own rule of never giving unwanted advice and urged her with some emotion: 'Get out! Get out as soon as you can! Don't make the same mistake as I did!'

We think we are proper people again, although naturally

our daughter will never regard us as anything other than Mum and Dad – that would be like finding out that your teacher has a first name or that your parents have had sex. I try to make a point of telling her about my past life (well, some of it, anyway) in the attempt to drum it into her head that I do have a separate existence from her. It's easier now that she has her own separate existence in the class-room and is used to me going to work, but I wonder whether she really grasps the fact that I have a rich inner life beyond the demands of work and domesticity. (What that rich inner life comprises I can't quite put my finger on at the moment, but I'm sure I would find it if I bothered to look hard enough.) But I shouldn't expect too much of her; it's dif-ficult, not to say impossible, for children to realise that the world doesn't revolve around them. I thought it was wonder-ful when my daughter first told me she loved me. The hormones made me want to blub. The brain cells told me she didn't have a clue what she was talking about and if called upon to prove her love would singularly fail to put herself into any danger, or even any mild physical discom-fort, in order to alleviate any suffering on my part, whereas I would crawl over burning coals to comfort her for the loss of a favourite hair slide. My suspicion that she was just saying what she thought I wanted to hear was confirmed when she went on to list all the other loves of her life including the cat, her new bed and cornflakes.

So when I started putting back together my other life as a human being, rather than just a parent, I didn't really expect her to take much notice. The fact that I could have been a world champion shot-putter or poet laureate would only be of interest to the extent that it impinged on her life. 'Oh no, not the Olympics again! How will I get my tea on time?' Among my numerous skills and talents the only one that has really impressed her (aside from being able to make a farty noise with my underarm) was the ability to touch-type. Really fast. I could be top billing at La Scala and it wouldn't be a tenth as exciting as being able to type with my eyes closed. And it felt quite good to have, at long last, inspired her with awe – especially after she had been so patronising about my rollerblading skills.

Another thing that (eventually) determined me to have a secret life away from my daughter was the fear of turning into a professional parent. I couldn't really see myself as one of those fun-loving types surrounded by a gaggle of small children. You never find them in a huddle with other mothers in the smokers' corner of the playground, bitching about bloody kids. They believe that having children is a joy, which it is, of course, but it's not a creed that I needed to live up to all my waking hours. I came across quite a few of these types when my daughter was small and I found them faintly spooky. Play is so important to them that they take a pride in their ability to join in childish games and behaviour.

'Oh, golly, look at me with sand in my hair again!' Always the first to join the children at any social gathering ('Oh, no, I'll have my wine later, we're just about to start a jolly game of hide-and-seek!') I always thought they were best left to get on with it while the rest of us finished the bottle and thanked God for a self-appointed entertainer to take the kids off our hands. Of course it's great for toddlers to have Mummy and Daddy involved in all their games, but it's the sort of parental behaviour that has to be curbed at all costs after a few short years. Teenagers tend to take a dim view of it. And unless you have a split personality or are a consummate actor there is the danger that playful Mummy persona will take over your whole life and you will find yourself becoming that silly sausage with the funny hat all the time. Permanently perky. Jesus. And the world will not only be passing you by, it will be taking a long detour in order to avoid you. I have to admit I'm relieved every time a children's television presenter is found snorting cocaine or having a three-in-a-bed romp – the idea that they might have *at all times* the jolly, inane personalities considered suitable for afternoon viewing is vaguely troubling. It could never have happened to John Noakes, of course. All those malicious rumours about Shep never amounted to anything, after all.

Too much involvement with children isn't healthy, I decided. It couldn't happen to me, surely, but there was always the anxiety at the back of my mind that one day, when questioned about world affairs, I would retort vapidly, 'Oh, we don't bother our heads about silly old wars, do we sweetheart?' I really did need to get out more.

I spent three and a half years looking after my girl full time. Three. And. A. Half. Years. That's a lot of swing-pushing and fish-finger-grilling. We were joined at the hip, shoulder, knee and elbow – there was nothing I didn't know about her physical and mental functions. Playgroup was my first taste of freedom, marred only slightly by her reluctance to go there. Anybody who has walked away from a sobbing child knows what a heartless cur it makes you feel, but I knew I had to do it. She was always happy as Larry when I went to pick her up, and I never got to the bottom of why she thought it necessary to fling herself around like an operatic heroine instead of just getting stuck into the sticklebricks straight away. When she had progressed to the sophisticated milieu of nursery school we passed by the scene of her desperate unhappiness one day and she remarked brightly 'Oh look, that's where I went to playgroup.' I asked her if she remembered why she cried when she got there and was met with a mystified look. Obviously all my fears about bullying, shyness and feelings of rejection were totally unfounded. She had just done it to make me feel bad.

But, with playgroup, then nursery, I was gradually

removing her limpet-like grasp on my life. So naturally, when the chance came to do something a little more challenging than figuring out how to get banana stains out of the upholstery I didn't hesitate to abandon her in favour of paid work – outside the house. I had once made the mistake of accepting some freelance work from my old boss. 'You'll be able to do it all from home over the telephone,' she assured me. When I got the brief I saw with horror that I would have to interview sixteen people. My boss had obviously never tried to make a phone call with a two-year-old in the house. Where do children get their inbuilt radar for dialling tones? As soon as I had got her involved in some quiet activity and started whispering questions into the receiver I would be interrupted with a loud 'Mummee!' It was just a nightmare, and more than once I felt like whimpering, 'What do you mean, he's in a meeting? Doesn't he realise *Teletubbies* is on?' I gave up with one woman, promising to ring her back the following day. When I did, I opened the interview with the very professional assurance 'It's OK, she's at playgroup.' I swore I would never again accept any work that I couldn't do unless my daughter was asleep, but leaving the house altogether was an even better option. I did wonder how she would react to the temporary disappearance of her personal slave, but it was about time we both enjoyed a little more independence. Especially me.

I worried that my first departure for work would be

hampered by having to beat off a screaming child clinging to my leg and begging me not to go. As if. Her dad was looking after her, so she barely gave me a second glance as I stole a last kiss and murmured plaintively, 'Bye, then.' She was playing with him at the time and I don't think she even bothered to reply. Admittedly I was wearing lipstick and a skirt, so she probably assumed that it was a complete stranger leaving the house and Mummy was upstairs having a lie down.

The journey was something I hadn't really thought about. I'd been going to work on London Transport for years and it hadn't occurred to me that successful tube travel was a skill that could be learned – and forgotten. I could negotiate a buggy round the obstacle course that passes itself off as a shopping centre, but I didn't know which end of the platform to stand and I felt a complete fraud. Commuters can detect weakness in fellow travellers and have no truck with ditherers. Looking at the signs or consulting a map marks you out as a rank amateur, deserving of a good buffet, which is exactly what I got. (I'm talking about malicious jostling rather than an attractive and appetising array of finger food.) After half an hour of tube travel I was seriously beginning to think that a playground full of two-year-olds really wasn't that bad: I was floundering in the world of work before I'd even started. It was only the instinct for self-preservation that got me to my destination, where I emerged into the light and breathed in lungfuls of the fresh air of central London. After a lengthy and productive cough I presented myself at the office – slightly battered and scared shitless. Maybe this is what it felt like to be abandoned by your mother to the terrors of the playgroup. I managed not to howl.

It was crunch time. My brain felt about as sharp and incisive as a wet nappy and my fingers, so dextrous when extracting splinters and wiping away snot, when presented with a keyboard turned into a bunch of sausages. Big fat slippery ones. Paper clips and swively chairs seemed, to my relief, to work in the same way as they always did. I even felt a faint rush of contempt when I found that photocopiers hadn't evolved much in my absence. I felt confident enough to do a complete revolution on my swivelly chair, but it only brought me right back face to face with the computer. Damn. There was nothing for it – after all I'd been through I would still have to do some proper work.

Going back to work is nothing like riding a bicycle. I might have felt a little wobbly at first, but I couldn't actually fall off a keyboard – give me a desk over a mountain bike any day of the week. I had returned to my proper milieu; I was perfectly able to concentrate, after all. Although I had been horrified to read, just before my daughter was born, that women's brains shrink during pregnancy, mine must have kept up with the rest of my body in gaining weight. It could also have been to do with the fact that absolutely nobody yelled 'Mummeee!' when I was in the middle of doing something. Not once. All day. It was bloody marvellous. Apart from absent-mindedly moving a pair of scissors to the back of the desk, out of the way of little fingers, I adapted back to office life remarkably quickly. This struck home at about four in the afternoon when I realised that I hadn't given my abandoned daughter a second thought since shutting the front door. Not only had I forgotten to bring in dozens of photographs for my colleagues to waste time cooing over, I hadn't been pining or fretting or phoning home every five minutes. What kind of a mother was I? A working one, obviously. Plus, I was getting *paid* for something I enjoyed doing. (Naturally a large portion of the first pay packet went on buying unnecessary guilt presents for my girl, but I soon knocked that on the head.)

My first day at work had been OK. It had been more than OK, it had been a positive success. I could still do stuff, my brain hadn't atrophied completely and I hadn't had any frantic calls to return home immediately because my daughter was inconsolable. As I scampered back to the bosom of my family, fizzing with pride and office gossip, I imagined the shrieks of delight that would greet my homecoming. They were waiting at the door for me. My husband, visibly shaken, was trying to work out how to lie down and drink heavily at the same time, and the house looked as if it had been the centre of a toy-bomb explosion. She had enjoyed his undivided attention all day long and had had an absolute ball, of course. She obviously couldn't wait for me to go away again, so no boring old housework would get in the way of her playtime. As I made a start on washing up the breakfast dishes I almost wished I was back in the office, where they have people to do that sort of thing.

It was only for a couple of days a week, after all, and there were benefits that I hadn't even thought of. In the early months I was always terribly well turned out for work, just because I was rediscovering all the clothes that had been left unworn in the wardrobe because they weren't suitable for sandpits. The joy of skirts! Lipstick! Earrings! A proper handbag that didn't contain wet wipes and spare socks! Going for a drink at lunchtime was bliss – athough I did feel as if I was doing something forbidden. I fully expected the mother-police to start sounding off sirens and that at any moment I would be asked to leave, and have to slink past the withering stares of legitimate drinkers who hadn't abandoned their children. Above all, reading on the train was a rediscovered pleasure – even if I had to do it standing up. Sitting at home and getting lost in a good yarn always seemed the height of decadence when there were so many other things to do, but now I had the perfect opport-unity to catch up on my reading.

It wasn't all unalloyed pleasure, of course. Often I had

rather longer to catch up on my reading than I cared for, when there was another signal failure or defective train. And after my first trouble-free departure from the house, my daughter soon cottoned on to the fact that this was going to be a regular occurrence and displayed considerable talent in preventing me from getting out of the door in the morning. Urgent requests for attention as the clock ticked meant that I invariably rushed out in a bad temper, wondering how, if I'd been up since six, it took two hours to get myself ready to leave. I got my come-uppance for that bad temper. One morning, in an irritable rush as usual, I grabbed an Ian McEwan paperback that I hadn't read before and stuffed it in my bag. *The Child in Time* starts with the disappearance of a three-year-old girl from a supermarket and the inconsolable grief of her parents. I reached work in tears and immediately had to phone home to apologise for not being very nice to my precious family. I've never been able to read that book. So much for being a hard-bitten career woman.

But as it was only for two days a week I soon encountered that Catch 22 that besets many part-time working mothers: a good portion of what I earned was instantly swallowed up by paying somebody else to look after my daughter when I wasn't there. As she got older and spent more time at school, my hours gradually increased – to the extent that now I long to be at home more often. Some people are never satisfied. But at least the novelty has worn off and I can now make it from bed to front door in about thirty minutes flat (although I'm not quite so well turned out as I used to be) and my daughter usually accepts my working life without a murmur. Although I am still subjected to the same circular conversations every so often when she decides to be clingy and difficult.

'I don't want you to go to work.'

'I don't want to go to work, but I have to.'

'Why?'

(Sings) 'To get you money to buy you things.'

'Off you go, then.'

I frequently take the opportunity to ram it home to her, when we are shopping or going to the cinema or eating pizza, that none of this would happen if I didn't go to work. Of course I will always be a mother first and foremost – especially in her opinion – but I can't help but be relieved that the days of round-the-clock childcare are over. Round-the-clock worry will never be over, naturally, but with my other life interests I can temper anxiety about the child with anxiety about my job and anxiety about my social life. That's what I call a rounded and fulfilled life.

Chapter Seven

Mother Substitutes

S O I DON'T HAVE TO DO ALL THE CHILDCARE myself any more, which is great. I have to find somebody else to do it. Not so great. Every mother has to hand her child over at some point, even if she keeps it tied to her apron strings until it goes to school, and it's not a pleasant experience. Putting your child in the care of another person throws up a whole new set of worries. How will my chosen carer cope in an emergency? Have I given her enough phone numbers and put all the neighbours on red alert? Are her references real? Did I remember to tell her about my daughter's favourite plate and how she likes her toast cut into little triangles? How much is too much information? Perhaps it would do the girl good to be looked after by somebody who says 'What's wrong with the blue one?'

instead of pandering to her every whim. But that would mean that somebody else was better at looking after her than I was! Relief at handing the job over for a while is always richly tinged with terror.

When our daughter was still under two I wouldn't have trusted Mother Teresa to look after her without my supervision (interference) but occasionally I needed to get her off my hands. So we crept gradually into childcare: employing somebody to come round for a couple of hours and keep her occupied while I painted the bedroom, for example. I'm not sure whether this gentle introduction to Mummy fading into the background was more for her benefit or mine, to tell the truth. I reasoned that if there were any major disasters I would still be on hand to sort them out, and it was an easy way of getting me used to letting go as well. But it didn't stop me from being troubled by feelings that it was vaguely immoral to pay another person to look after your child while you were still in the house. If I was a proper mother I should be able to look after a toddler and decorate the walls at the same time, surely? 'Not without some rather unpleasant paint-based incidents,' friends assured me, so I felt mollified. I wasn't ditching my responsibility after all – I was just trying to get the painting done in relative safety. She had a great time playing, but my decorating was subject to constant interruptions because she knew I was still around and was highly skilled at making unreasonable demands at the most inconvenient moments. I should have admired her ability to be so manipulative at such a young age; in fact I was just a bit irritated.

Getting a part-time job necessitated putting things on a rather more formal footing, and a childminder seemed the most obvious solution. London is crawling with childminders, you can't throw a stick without hitting at least three and a couple of pre-schoolers to boot, so it was just a question of getting a list from the council and making my choice. A childminder would be perfect: trained and vetted and probably more skilled at and experienced in childcare than I was. Plus, my daughter would be socialising with other children and not wrecking my house with her toys. As soon as I had made the decision the papers seemed suddenly to be full of stories of freak accidents, unqualified charlatans and worse – I swear they were doing it on purpose just to frighten me.

Even if they weren't evil-minded predators childminders might exert influences that I wouldn't approve of. Like watching *Pokémon*-style cartoons or talking about 'puppy-dogs' or 'toothie-pegs'. Regretting my lack of a wide network of friends and relations in close proximity I pushed to the back of my mind stories of cruelty and neglect and listened to friends with 'treasures'. 'Well, on paper she's a nightmare: she's got a dog and she smokes, but she's absolutely fantastic with the kids.' 'I just couldn't want anybody better than Barbara, I have every confidence in her. We were so lucky to find her.' Perhaps I should have listened a bit harder to that last sentence. After several dispiriting phone calls and visits I realised that luck does play quite a large part in finding suitable childcare. Childminders are a bit like poolside sun loungers: all the best ones are taken. I never did find anybody I particularly liked, let alone would trust with my child, so we had to do a rethink. Having convinced myself that a childminder would be ideal, I now had to refute all my own arguments and decide that it was probably all for the best and our daughter would be happier in her own home anyway. If nothing else, motherhood is a constant lesson in pragmatism.

We decided to pay somebody to come to our house and look after our daughter for the few hours before and after nursery. I might not have a wide network of friends and relations on hand, but we can draw on a pretty wide network of young Czech girls living in London – which eventually proved quite fruitful. Just when we were in despair, I was due to start work in less than a fortnight and we had no childcare at all, Nikola came into our lives. She had intended to go home, but she would do us a favour and stay on for a few weeks while we sorted ourselves out.

The first time I came home from work I walked into a kitchen that was cleaner than it had been for months and I nearly cried. 'Well, I had nothing to do while she was at nursery,' Nikola remarked with a shrug. I wanted to fall on her neck and sob my thanks. Our daughter was having a whale of a time – neighbours commented on how much they seemed to enjoy themselves in the playground – I was relaxed and happy and didn't have any concerns about leaving my daughter in somebody else's care. Even the tongue stud didn't spoil Nikola's perfection. It couldn't last, of course. I was paying this experienced, charming, intelligent (tongue stud excepted), caring woman a pittance to look after my child and I couldn't expect her to do it for very long. She had a career on hold and was destined for far better things than cleaning my kitchen. I would have done well to remember that when considering future employees. All the girls who came to look after our daughter were fine, but Nikola stood out like a good deed in a naughty world. I just needed to find another person like her. With my hours set to increase, we had to review our *ad hoc* arrangements and get things a little more settled. After considering all the alternatives, we eventually decided our best option would be to get an au pair. Looking back, I'm not sure which set us slithering down the steepest learning curve: having a baby or having an au pair. Yes, I do know that you are supposed to go *up* a learning curve.

We knew all about au pairs. The hours of slavery, tyrannical parents and even more tyrannical children. Homesickness, hunger, mutual hatred – some of these girls have an absolutely torrid time. Having had a friend's daughter sleeping on our floor after she had left a house where she had been groped by a lay preacher, we were quite well aware that it's not much of a job, as jobs go. So with us it was going to be different. The work wasn't onerous, she would have plenty of free time – and we were such nice people! What could possibly go wrong? We would get a Czech, so she wouldn't feel quite so divorced from home and would help with our daughter's language. We would also get somebody recommended by a friend so there would always be a connection, rather than getting a complete stranger through an agency. I didn't want anybody too young, and she had to be capable and sensible, of course. Somewhere out there was another Nikola.

After all the care we took, all the precautions and sensible advice we listened to, I still don't quite know how we ended up with the Anti-Nikola. Sheer bloody ignorance, probably. Au pairs and families are like landlords and tenants. For every grasping, lazy, unpleasant landlord there is a destructive, criminally minded tenant. After a while living with our first au pair I began to think I would willingly give myself up to be groped by a lay preacher. She lasted six months, and I think if she had been our second or third au pair, instead of our first, she would have lasted about six days. We just didn't know what we were doing. She knew exactly what she was doing and we were tyrannised unmercifully. In my pitiful naïvety I only heard faint tinklings when I should have been deafened by alarm bells.

It's a much more complex relationship than we had been led to believe. The best thing about having an au pair is that you have someone always on hand, living in your house. The worst thing about having an au pair is that you have someone always on hand, living in your house. And they are supposed to be a member of the family – but they're not. Anybody you live with is bound to irritate you at some point, and if it is a loved one you don't hesitate to bawl them out and generally make your feelings known. A colleague illustrated the point exactly. Her latest au pair had a habit of clumping noisily up the stairs in heavy shoes, until she could feel her neck muscles tensing as soon as the au pair started heading for the staircase. If it was your own daughter doing that you would just yell 'Will you take your bloody shoes off!' but it's the last thing you can do to an au pair. With one of ours, I would probably have been rewarded with pained expressions, sulks and accusations of bullying. I might have got exactly the same reaction from my daughter, but at least I could just ignore it. But if au pairs are not really members of the family, they're not really employees either. Neither fish nor fowl, but sometimes foul.

After our first disaster we had another review and identified our mistakes, which were legion. For a start, I wouldn't be so dogmatic about age. I still didn't want a nineteen-year-old, but being twenty-six doesn't necessarily mean that you are more experienced, capable and sensible. It might mean that if you are approaching thirty and want to be an au pair you are shiftless, lacking in direction and can't think of anything better to do with your life except live at somebody else's expense. Nikola was so good because she was over-qualified. And we really had to be stricter about rules. It was definitely our fault if we didn't make the boundaries clear, so we would write down duties, and instead of blithely expecting somebody to make our daughter a meal from what she could find in the fully stocked fridge and freezer, provide her with a detailed menu every day. Oh, and we really should find somebody who actually liked children. With those decisions agreed on, we decided to trust to hope over experience and have another go. It still took another few false starts, failures and 'serious talks' before we settled into it. Au pairs are all different, with different strengths and weaknesses, so once we had decided on the rules we soon realised that you have to change them every time to accommodate vastly contrasting personalities and skills. If one was useless at housework she was excellent at making paper hats; but the next one might be a whiz with a J-cloth, so I shouldn't automatically prise the floor mop from her fingers and hand her a crayon instead.

It's too often a relationship based on mutual resentment. First of all, I had to overcome my resentment of somebody else coming into my house, taking over my job and my kitchen. When I could shut the door on a childminder at the end of a day I didn't mind so much my daughter pointing out that 'We never make animals out of conkers and matchsticks!' With somebody in the house all the time, I was uneasy about getting sidelined. So there are areas that remain firmly out of the domain of any au pair. Bathtime, bedtime and getting ready for school are exclusively her parents' responsibility. Which cuts down the hours that an au pair has to work, of course, so I would occasionally feel faint inklings of resentment that there was somebody in our home who was having a much easier life than either of us. And in our spare bedroom as well. I'm afraid it still rankles with me that there is a room in our house that I have never actually used myself. I've only ever been in there to decorate it or clean it so somebody else can make use of it. And leave it in a shocking state at times. I hardly ever went into the au pair's room – the sight of all those cuddly toys cluttering up my tasteful furnishings just turned my stomach. And I really objected to a large poster of Russell Crowe on the *outside* of the door – but I didn't say anything, of course. And when the relationship isn't working I especially resent the fact that I'm made to feel like a domestic dictator because I am reluctant to take on another person's sometimes non-existent problems. After living with au pairs we found out that we weren't nice people after all. We harboured murderous thoughts. Instead of looking for the good in people we spent more time than was healthy standing around in the kitchen bitching. We hid chocolate.

There is a wonderful children's book by Norton Juster called *The Phantom Tollbooth*, which I'm saving up for my daughter. At the end the hero has to escape through the Mountains of Ignorance, which are crawling with demons such as the Gorgons of Hate and Malice, the Overbearing Know-it-All, the Gross Exaggeration and the Threadbare Excuse. The last is a small, pathetic creature that goes about mumbling 'I've not been well…I missed the bus…But the page was torn out…' and so on. It looks harmless and friendly enough but once it grabs you it hardly ever lets go. After a particularly fraught couple of months I began to believe that these monsters were not fictional characters at all. Each and every one of them has at some time come down off the mountain to be employed as our au pair.

Of course they resent me too for all sorts of reasons, some valid, some not. English grammar is not my fault, but they all seemed to hold me personally responsible for it. One was very strict about my timekeeping. She would make a great show of looking at her watch and rushing off if I was ten minutes late back from work. Six o'clock was her knocking-off time and that was it, I was on my own after that. It was the same girl who was consistently late picking up our daughter from school, so obviously her watch only worked at certain times of the day. Some of them seemed to resent even doing the job at all, and when I found myself paying through the nose to get my daughter into a holiday club at half-term because the au pair didn't want to miss her daytime English classes, I thought we had learned very little from our previous mistakes.

But no matter how awful they might think I am, some of them have been awful to me as well. I've suffered hypochondria, bulimia and even a possible case of hypothermia when one forgot her key and 'didn't want to wake us up' so decided to sleep on the garden bench. The fact that she didn't have hypothermia would seem to suggest that she hadn't actually been there all night but probably arrived home very shortly before she woke us up at five. But I dare say that's just me being nasty and suspicious. And you can't accuse us of fobbing our daughter off with childcare on the cheap when you add in the cost of phone bills, a new phone, new crockery, replacement taps in the bathroom and an entire freezer full of food when one au pair left the door open.

Of course it hasn't been all bad. I've never had to worry about my husband having an affair with a pert young thing, for example. Murdering one of them, yes, sleeping with any of them, never. And through it all the childcare has usually been good. After the very first gorgon, whom our daughter refused even to call by name (she used to call her 'somebody else') she's never had reason to complain. Obviously my daughter is a much nicer person than I am, because she had no trouble getting on with her au pairs, but I probably wouldn't have done either if they hadn't been lodged under my roof.

We've settled into a routine now with which we are all fairly happy. Only 'fairly' happy? Well, is there a single person in the universe who I think would look after my daughter better than I do? I'm constantly torn between wanting some time for myself and wanting to take over the job entirely. I can even question the professionals sometimes. I was in my daughter's classroom once when she remarked 'Oh, cool.' I immediately responded 'Cool? Where do you get these expressions from?' and her young Australian teacher admitted: 'Er, probably from me, actually.' In all other respects he was an excellent teacher, I just wish he wouldn't say 'Cool'. I had no objection at all to them singing 'A koala up a gum tree' to the tune of 'The Twelve Days of Christmas' for the annual concert, but 'Cool'? Too late now, of course, and all attempts to make a five-year-old say 'Oh, how splendid' have fallen on stony ground. Still, it doesn't really matter, worse things could happen. And they do, unfortunately, which is when my parental worry circuits go into overdrive.

As I turned the corner into my street one evening I was faced with a crowd of neighbours and a small figure lying under a blanket by the roundabout in the playground. All my internal organs turned to jelly and didn't solidify again until I had determined that the small figure wasn't my daughter. The shame at my relief that it was somebody else's daughter wasn't pleasant, but I suppose it was natural. The little girl in question played there every day with her childminder and by some horrible fluke on this afternoon had fallen awkwardly off the roundabout and broken her leg – in full view of not only her childminder but her mother and grandmother as well. It was a nasty accident that probably couldn't have been prevented, but her childminder admitted to me that she was 'bloody glad' that her mother had been present at the time.

At times like these the most professional, experienced childcare expert isn't as good as Mum. Even if Mum's face is ashen, it's the face that the child wants to see through its tears. That's what I like to think, anyway, even if I secretly wonder if I would have been any damn use at all if the figure under the blanket had been related to me, and I would have been very relieved to have some calm and competent aid. While the neighbours waited for the ambulance, I rushed inside and put the fear of God into my daughter and the au pair with another long and detailed lecture about the importance of being careful on the play equipment and the superiority of board games over any sort of outdoor activity that involves anything other than walking slowly while holding firmly on to somebody's hand. After a brief period as star of the playground in pink plaster cast and wheelchair, the little girl is now fine, but she did cause me to do some serious calculations about whether I could afford to give up work entirely.

But I can't, so there are going to be a good few years yet ahead of us during which our daughter will have to be in the care of teachers, au pairs, childminders or relatives until she can look after herself. She is already asking how old she has to be before she can go to the shops on her own and I try to answer truthfully and not growl 'About twenty-three if your father has anything to do with it.' The time will come, but we haven't told her that when it does we are planning to get a very large, fierce dog. At least I can train it to take its shoes off before it runs upstairs.

Chapter Eight

Mess is more

IT'S ONE OF THE FIRST THINGS THAT THE BOOKS will tell you about ensuring a happy and harmonious family life. Get organised. In this case they may, in fact, have a point. It's no good being a brilliant storyteller for your kids if, in your little world of creative play, you forget to feed them. There are some things that you really have to put at the top of your 'to do' list. Likewise, all children are under the impression that Ariel is indeed an airy spirit which does all the washing by magic. So they will cut up pretty rough if school uniforms, sports kit and favourite T-shirts are not magically back in the wardrobe within hours of being dropped in grubby heaps on the bedroom floor. One thing I did like about being at home all day with a small child was that, beyond feeding and sleeping, and remembering to turn on the television in time for Noddy, there was never any necessity for rigid routines. By the time she was at school and I was back at work, however, morning times took on a very different colour. Unfortunately, there was now an obligation to get dressed before noon – and in the right clothes. I would have to get my act together a little more efficiently.

But it's one thing managing to get dressed before noon, quite another to have a clean and happy house that runs like clockwork. Given that having small children and getting organised are mutually exclusive concepts, how far should I take my military training in rota-writing before giving up and disappearing under the tidal wave of chaos that passes as a normal family home?

A great part of the chaos in this particular household is caused by the extraordinary amount of stuff that one small child can accumulate. I wouldn't have thought it possible that someone so small needs such enormous quantities of kit in order to function properly, but yet again, I was wrong.

Even though I tried to keep baby equipment to a minimum, there seemed to be an awful lot of it. All of it plastic and ugly and in a hideous shade of aqua, unknown in the natural world, for which I have developed a deep and abiding hatred. Steriliser, bottles, changing mat, potty, giant packs of nappies, high chair, low chair, bouncy chair – how relieved I was when each milestone was passed and another piece of baby paraphernalia could be consigned to the bin or the Oxfam shop. And then, when she was still under two we moved from a two-bedroomed flat to a four-bedroomed house (not bragging, just stating a fact – what we gained in space we lost in postcode status). I couldn't wait – just think of the oodles of room we were going to have! I imagined vast acres of space unsullied by playpens, gleaming surfaces without bottles of gripe water or teething rings decorating them, not having to walk into rooms sideways. This was my chance to get really organised. In a few months all the baby stuff would be gone and we could get back to a normal environment. What was I thinking of?

Baby equipment is *nothing*. The amount of stuff that a small child considers essential to life would fill a warehouse. For a start there are the toys. Our daughter had a lovely room when she was tiny, full of elegantly crafted and attractive toys for babies, all vetted by her parents, of course. She couldn't speak so she couldn't object when I was completely ruthless with anything I didn't like. We were secretly and hopelessly trying to influence her taste, but I think even then we knew deep down that we were on a losing wicket. Since we have lost all control over her choice of playthings she will reject anything that I even vaguely like the look of and pounce with delight on hideously coloured plastic guff. Why are so many of the world's limited resources dedicated to the production of fairy princess plastic tiaras and totally useless things to put on the tops of pencils? Doesn't China have any other exports? Why is it all so tiny and pointless and easily lost? (Or, not easily enough if you look at it another way.)

But it's not all pink and plastic – quite a lot of it is squashy and furry. I don't think we have ever bought our daughter a soft toy in her entire puff, we've never had to. We have swarming herds of the things, all with their own names and places in the social structure of the toybox. Our daughter is a favourite with a neighbour who is a car boot sale addict. One day she saw her in the playground with a stuffed cat, so bought her another one, then another one. I would have thought that one stuffed cat was enough for anyone, but she now has eight. Polly, Poppy, Harriet, Mummy Cat, Daddy Cat, Auntie Cat, Bob and Shunkula (don't ask, I have no idea). Naturally I can't get rid of any of them because I would be breaking up the feline family. And it doesn't stop with cats. As well as all the dolls, we've got dogs, rabbits, several giraffes, bears (both brown and white), hippos, birds, lions – the entire fauna of several continents in fact, plus some unidentifiable beasts with stripes and clothes. We even have a stuffed ant (it's a Czech thing) and a stuffed mosquito (it was a holiday jabs thing). All of them shoved into a jumbo-sized toybox and hardly ever played with. No point in Daddy muttering darkly about his bleak childhood in communist Czechoslovakia and only having one toy monkey and bloody glad of it. I tried to look on the bright side and pointed out that in lieu of soft toys he used to smuggle live animals into the flat. His mother might not have had to fight her way through fun fur to get into the bedroom, but she did have to dispose of the odd mouse or hedgehog corpse. I'm not allowed to dispose of anything, especially since that bad moment I had when she passed by the window of the charity shop and said brightly 'Oh look – I've got one like that.' Not any more, you haven't, but don't worry, there's plenty more acrylic crocodiles where that one came from.

I learned my lesson and will now ask her regularly to go through her own toybox and find things she doesn't want any more. It never amounts to more than one or two items, but I daren't make the choices myself. I've known middle-aged successful professional types suddenly reveal deep-seated mental scars caused by the casual binning of some moth-eaten rabbit when they were five. This stuff rankles.

But if my daughter rarely plays with her squidgy menagerie, she is by no means inactive around the house. If she ever becomes a famous artist I may regret chucking out about three million quids' worth of precious early works, but it's a risk I'm willing to take rather than be buried by bits of daubed paper, like Robert de Niro in *Brazil*. I have to do that in secret, as well. If she catches me tiptoeing round the house with a bin bag she demands to check the contents, fishes out two yoghurt pots and a toothpick and complains 'What's my boat doing in the rubbish?' Charles Saatchi himself couldn't find the space to display all of her prodigious output, so I have a special box I pretend to keep all her artwork in. I fillet it out regularly, but even I am not often ruthless enough to chuck in the bin a picture of a smiling face with 'I love you mummy' scrawled across it in wobbly letters. I keep meaning to paper a room with it all, but the weight of Blu-Tack would probably take the plaster off the walls. And naturally she need the tools to produce all this work. Not just a packet of felt tips and some pencils. We must have close to three thousand coloured pencils in this house (that's only a very slight exaggeration) – yet strangely you can never find a decent sharpener when you need one, even though I seem to remember buying dozens of the things.

She works in 3D as well. You know why it's called junk modelling? It *is* junk. I've never seen a princess's castle with 'I can't believe it's not butter!' written up the side, but it's her work so has to take pride of place on the dining-room table. I can't even throw genuine rubbish away these days, let alone the odd toy. Apparently, she 'needs' every toilet roll, kitchen paper tube, any packaging with pictures, bits of bubble wrap, cardboard box and yoghurt pot that I had assumed was surplus to requirements. Our daughter seems to have adapted the old army maxim to her own use: 'If it moves, play with it; if it doesn't move, paint it.' (Then glue it to something else and leave it in the middle of the floor.)

As well as toys and artwork, there are also the items that come under the heading of 'miscellaneous treasures'. My sitting room is filled with elegant antique furniture and precious objets d'art (Ikea certainly is a wonder, isn't it?). One day I happened to glance around and realised that my stylish and expertly chosen furnishings had been supplemented by a miniature sombrero full of pine needles, diseased-looking pigeon feathers stuck into every plant pot, a small pile of gravel and six – no, seven – decorated toilet rolls. Her latest fad is collecting grass seeds because she's going to use them 'to make things'. It might be possible to organise bank statements and kitchen utensils, but even I am hard put to cope with grass-seed-and-small-bits-of-leaf storage. There doesn't seem to be a section for it in the Ikea catalogue. Where are the surfaces? What happened to the acres of space? How much smaller can this house get before we are crushed beneath the weight of our daughter's possessions?

When she was a little younger, any trip to the park made me feel like a nineteenth-century naturalist. I should have taken collecting boxes, specimen bottles and at least one pack animal. Instead I always ended up with pockets full of dead flowers, conkers, pine cones, seeds and sticks. I know this is just normal child behaviour, and had to laugh one day when I passed another buggy in the park. The mother pushing it remarked to me 'Got enough sticks, then?' and I noticed that she was laden down with enough wood for a sizeable log cabin. Perhaps she used hers to build a small shed to house all her child's acquisitions. I used to surreptitiously drop mine when my daughter wasn't looking, but she burst into tears one day when I flatly refused to drag home a fallen branch the size of a lamp-post. Apparently it was more essential childhood equipment.

I now know that you don't get rid of all the accessories that go with a small baby, you just swap them for more accessories for children. It was a happy day when the buggy finally went, but I didn't gain any space because it was very soon replaced with bike, scooter, friends' bikes – so the hall now looks like a pit stop for the junior Tour de France and there's barely room to hang your coat up. I thought that children just ran about playing, but they can't do it without a vast array of special apparatus. The latest must-have is a pair of rollerblades (plus knee pads, elbow pads, wrist guards and helmet) but I don't know how long they are going to stay in favour. As I tried to hear myself think above the noise of about seventeen kids rollerblading up and down the road outside my house, some bright spark appeared with a pogo stick. Sure enough, five minutes later daughter comes skating up to me crying excitedly, 'Mummy! Did you see...' No. Absolutely not. *Forget it!*

Having a girl seems to involve even more essential lifestyle accessories. She has more clothes, shoes and handbags than I do. Nail varnish and body glitter are *de rigueur* now for any girl over three, and her hair adornments would fill a small skip (although try finding two hairclips that match first thing in the morning when we're late for school). I dread every Christmas and birthday because however much of this stuff she has, she's going to get more, 'because little girls love all these things'. Yes, they do, but their mothers could certainly do without them. The first time she had a birthday that she knew about, I made a serious miscalculation in the present-giving department. I actually enjoyed buying her little girly accoutrements and actively sought out sparkle. I hadn't reckoned on all the things that she would get from other people, of course, and it all amounted to quite a sizeable haul. How do other parents stem this tide of stuff? Confiscate three-quarters of presents as soon as they arrive in the house? Or do I have a particular problem because my girl is so stupendously popular that she receives ten times as many presents as any other kid? I'd like to think so, but another explanation is that I seem to have a lot of friends with sons, who can't wait for an excuse to be let loose in Claire's Accessories.

My house is just getting smaller and smaller, but apparently this is my fault for not being organised enough. (Or ruthless enough, evidently.) I have a special circle of hell reserved for writers on household style. Unfortunately, although I hate all those magazines I also have a terrible addiction to them and can't quite kick the habit of buying one occasionally. It's usually because I've been foolishly seduced by that perfidious cover line: 'Clever storage solutions', but I don't know why, because it always ends in tears: me with a red pen and a Stanley knife defacing pages of 'stylish and practical' children's rooms. (Here's a clever storage solution for you: get rid of a load of stuff and put what's left in a cupboard. There you are, there's a rainforest saved and about half a million stylists on the dole. Everybody wins.) I don't know why I torture myself by looking at pictures of other people's elegant Georgian family homes, vainly trying to spot the piles of Kinder toys, cracker novelties, feather collections, bits of precious paper, discarded socks and unwashed paintbrushes. They don't exist in other people's houses. But no matter how often I read it, written as gospel, I am coming to the conclusion that in real life 'stylish and practical' is an oxymoron of massive proportions. Three-year-old twins Sam and Ella undoubtedly have a lovely bedroom, tastefully and stylishly decorated and looking superb in the photos, but I don't know how Sam and Ella feel about being tied to chairs all day. That's the only explanation I can find for these fantasy family homes. I stare and stare at the photos but can never bring myself to believe that these houses are home to one or more small children. Maybe they aren't. Maybe the kids are kept in kennels in the extensive grounds so their parents can enjoy unchipped skirting boards and pale cream sofas. My daughter only has to walk into a room to make it look untidy, but I don't think she's particularly abnormal. In my experience, one small child can make more mess than a party full of middle-aged drunks with no substantial hold on the finger buffet. Things get spilt, crumbled, dropped and broken with wearisome regularity, but that's normal, isn't it? Or are my floors a bit crunchy underfoot because I'm just not strict enough?

I've spent too long now picking up and tidying and generally trying to create order out of chaos. I have occasionally tried the old standby of 'Well, if you kept your things a bit tidier you would *know* where Barbie's shoe is', but frankly I'm fighting a losing battle. What I should have been doing was laying down the law: you *will* put your toys away, clean your room and eat a biscuit without covering the carpet knee-deep in crumbs. There will be no magic sand on the sofa, Play-Doh in the kitchen or rubber snakes in my bed because I don't want them there. End of argument. This is the sort of old-school style of parenting that everyone hankers after and wants for their own children. Obedience and respect and strict observance of the rules, just like in Granny's day. It would make life easier, of course, if my household was run on strict military lines, but although I might now remember Granny with admiration and respect, when I was a kid all her sodding rules and regulations were a royal pain. When I was five I'm sure I thought it was supremely unimportant whether I hung my coat up or slung it on the floor. I had better things to do than make hospital corners on my bed or put my shoes in a neat row, so I can hardly blame my daughter now if she shows signs of having inherited her mother's sluttishness. I also remember a schoolfriend whose mother was heavily into plastic covers and coasters and wiping down all the kitchen surfaces every time somebody walked into the room. Their house was a picture but the woman was *completely* neurotic and drove the whole family mad. That's my excuse for not being a domestic goddess.

So I suppose I'll just continue to pick up and wipe down after my daughter until she grows into a tidy teenager with a passion for doilies. Or, more likely, in fifteen years' time instead of carefully smoothed out sweet wrappers and crushed paper chains I shall be clearing her room of empty wine bottles and mouldy coffee cups. No doubt if that happens I shall only have myself to blame.

Meanwhile, if I can't keep the clutter in order I can at least organise the running of our lives around it. It's called 'juggling' – I've heard about it on *Woman's Hour*. Some people can manage it astonishingly well, although when a high-powered City executive with three small children is interviewed in her spotless state-of-the-art kitchen and murmurs 'It's all a question of getting organised' I suspect that what she really means is that it's all a question of paying other people to get you organised. Not being in a position to do that, I can't decide whether I'm any good at running a household or not. Saint or slut? Which is me?

Since our daughter was born my brain has been in a constant whirl of calculations and sketchy planning – with the occasional disastrous lapse of memory.

- If I cook this while she's asleep then I can feed her when she wakes up and still have enough to freeze for tomorrow.

- If we take a different route to the playcentre I can nip into the doctor's on the way and go past a postbox.

- I can get a whole section of wall painted if she sits through the whole of Teletubbies, so I'd better prepare the area before it starts.

- I must wear that shirt to work because I'll be doing a white wash on Thursday. I have to do it on Thursday because she's running out of school clothes.

And so on, and so on until I think my brain has turned into a complex grid of pigeon-holes that all have to be filled in the right order otherwise the whole structure will collapse.

Four school shirts and five days in the week is one that

always trips me up. Why don't I just get another shirt? Because the ones with the school badge on are only available from her school, and I always forget, or don't take my purse with me, or the Welfare office is closed, or they don't have her size... I'll just put another wash on. I consider it a great achievement that only once in her school life have I had to send her in a white T-shirt because I miscalculated the washing rota. But then, I consider it a great achievement that we are washed, fed and clothed after a fashion: if I manage to scrape the pizza off the oven more than once a year I think I deserve a medal for services to the house.

On a good day at home I think I've done well if I've tidied up, put the washing on, done some work, posted bills and remembered to buy a birthday card. Then the dread phrase strikes: 'What are we going to eat tonight?' Somehow it never conveys the idea of 'Which delicious concoction from our vast repertoire of dishes shall we enjoy on this fine evening?' It always smacks of 'What the *hell* are we going to eat tonight?' Grabbing something from Sainsbury's on the way home from work is probably not the action of a domestic goddess, but we do eventually get fed, so I suppose that counts as juggling – or is it just throwing one ball up in the air and catching it clumsily?

It's true that if I spent less time poking despondently at the contents of the shed and actually took half a day to clear it out it would probably improve the quality of my life just a little. If I sorted out the kitchen cupboards instead of just cramming stuff in and shutting the doors really quickly I wouldn't waste time trying to find things among the jumble. It might sound a little sad, but I actually enjoy getting things clean and tidy (oven excepted). I would love to have a month dedicated entirely to arranging drawers, cleaning pictures and scrubbing out cupboards. (Not to mention re-pointing the brickwork and fixing the guttering and doing some serious downsizing in the soft toy department.) I want some day to have a household that runs like a well-oiled machine, with a place for everything and everything in its place. However, with the grubby business of earning money uppermost in my mind, housework becomes a displacement activity. I always have a clean, ironed T-shirt to hand when getting ready for work, but it saddens me (yes, really) that I have to take it out of a drawer that is not tidily colour-co-ordinated and bears evidence of the cat having slept in it. The kitchen cupboards are well stocked but not well ordered. Nothing is quite good enough for the impossibly high standards I would like to uphold if I just had the time and the right mental attitude. We all know that housework expands to fill the time available to do it, so if I did have nothing else to do I would probably find myself scrubbing the doorstep and polishing cake forks, but without going that far, it would be nice if things were a little less slapdash. Does that make me a frustrated perfectionist or just terribly anal with an inability to prioritise? I don't know. I'd just like to be able to get to the back of the shed.

I think what would really help me would be the opportunity to take a good hard look at somebody else's domestic set-up. I *notice* if my skirting boards are dusty, but I never look at them in anybody else's house. In any apparently well-ordered home I suspect I would, on close examination, find unwashed sheets, jumbles of bank statements and electricity bills, dust balls under the sofa, lists of forgotten birthdays, rotting food at the back of the fridge and cutlery drawers full of crumbs. I hope I never do get the opportunity to do some serious snooping, just in case I find out that other people actually *do* iron their sheets and never run out of milk.

I'll never be as organised as I would like to be. It could be something to do with the fact that when I should be sewing on nametapes, *Midsomer Murders* is on and all I want to do is lie about on the sofa scoffing at John Nettles in order to convince myself that I do have some critical faculties left. (I know, too easy.) But I can scrape by, sometimes by the skin of my teeth, admittedly, with the aid of a calendar and some Post-It notes. Wednesday: library book; Thursday: PE kit; Friday: spelling test; every day: lunchbox; Saturday: leotard; Sunday: karate outfit with a funny name that I can never remember but it doesn't matter as long as it's clean – it's not too much to cope with. I don't know how people with more than one child actually do it all. With two or three timetables to keep in mind I would probably just grind to a halt.

I'll have to leave the kitchen cupboards for that mythical era in the future when I have more time. By then the contents will have crumbled to dust all by themselves anyway, so they'll just need a quick wipe with a J-cloth. When I'm in my dotage I shall probably enjoy spending long winter evenings putting photographs into albums and arranging CDs in alphabetical order, but until then the best I can hope for is just to keep a superficial sense of regularity. As far as my own household is concerned I shall probably have to boil down 'getting organised' to a few basics:

- Hiring a skip every so often, or getting a lock-up garage
- Never running out of her favourite foods
- Writing down significant dates such as birthdays, doctor's appointments, school start dates and carol concerts on the calendar
- Looking at the calendar sometimes
- Wearing blinkers round the house

Sorted.

Chapter Nine

No contest

I'VE GOT TO STOP BUYING THOSE HOMES
magazines, they only upset me. But even if I can come
to terms with the fact that my bed just has a duvet on it, not
a tactile combination of sumptuous silks, satins and
woollens for a luxurious layered feel, there are plenty of
other areas in life where I fall vastly short of my aspirations.
What's the difference between healthy competition and a
bitter struggle for supremacy? When the object of the
contest is a child. While trying hard to come to terms with
myself as a mother, there was also the small fact of my
daughter's existence. If I was struggling with my new role,
how was she coping with the business of life? How did
she compare to other children, and should I even be
thinking about comparisons?

Here we have one of those contradictions that crop up
so often in the busy and glamorous life of any parent. We all

hug to our bosoms the secret knowledge that our kids are the best in the world and the baby Jesus doesn't even come close in terms of sheer perfection. Would you ever describe your child as average? I know that my girl could knock any other kid in the world into a cocked hat in terms of talent, intelligence, beauty, comedic skills and physical prowess. She's a great girl, and I've got several long and fascinating videos to prove it, but I try not to ram it down people's throats too much. (Actually, I do try, but people stop me, for some reason.) Despite this secret knowledge, however, I spend more of my waking hours than is good for me fretting about whether she really is doing all right. Am I doing all right? Is the woman down the road doing better? Should I stick pins in her perfect bloody kid?

Most of the time this churning mass of contradictory thought is kept under control by the thin veneer of societal mores. When mixing with other parents and their children we engage in the politeness gavotte. You praise other people's children and disparage your own, even encouraging other mothers in their ludicrous belief in their children's superiority – and they do the same to you. 'Oh, no. My Tom is terrible at going to bed, I'm sure your Amy is much better about it,' we simper collectively. We're all lying. We know we are lying, they know they are lying but we carry on the pretence because that's what you do. A slight change in emphasis, however, and parental protectiveness goes into overdrive. Should anyone break the rules of the gavotte and dare to criticise – however faintly – my own child, all pretence is stripped away and replaced by simmering rage. 'Stupid woman! How could she say that when she barely knows my girl. At least my child never behaves like a rampaging elephant in her house. What *that* child needs is a little less self-expression and a little more discipline…' and so on and so on, until the rage passes and I can again take comfort in the secret knowledge that no kid on earth is better than my own. Even quite innocent remarks such as 'She's such a little thing, isn't she?' will immediately have me on the alert, ready to defend. 'She's not big. None of us is big. What of it?' I know somebody with a daughter almost exactly the same age as mine, but at least a head taller. This woman is obviously proud of her girl's height and secretly feels sorry for me for having such a little runt. I, on the other hand, thank God I haven't spawned a beanpole and rejoice in my daughter's daintiness. Ludicrous, isn't it? We're both right and both wrong (but I get some brilliant cast-off clothes).

Some parents don't understand the rules of the gavotte and really overstep the mark when it comes to competition, although nobody will admit to it. They will call themselves encouraging, interested, concerned – anything but what everyone else calls them: bloody pushy. Their poor kids can't be left alone to build a sandcastle without a lesson in architecture. And despite their obsession with their own kids' achievements, don't think yours will escape their scrutiny – everyone is measured on a scale of their own devising. After all, there's no point in having a genius child unless you can hold him up as an example to the bunch of dolts that constitutes his peer group. Truly pushy parents, the ones who swear by womb music and flashcards and Suzuki lessons, will ever be on the receiving end of my deepest contempt. I would never *dream* of being like that – a house full of books and some discreet help with homework is quite enough for a child of five to get a good start in life. Hothousing is what you do to delicate little plants, not delicate little children, and there's no way in the world that I would try to mould my daughter into something she's not.

Although she does do dance classes. And karate lessons. And we're thinking about a musical instrument. But we are absolutely not pushy. I stoutly maintain that I shell out cash for these things just so long as she enjoys doing them and it really is immaterial whether she is any good or not. Although it would be *nice* if she showed some talent. I try very hard to quash the feelings I get when taking a peek at her dancing class – complicated feelings that range from a glow of maternal pride when she performs some graceful action, through irritation when she scratches her bum straight afterwards, to vague jealousy when another child does better than she does and, worst of all, completely inexcusable satisfaction that at least she's not as hopeless as *that* kid. I'm not pushy. I'm not pushy. I'm not pushy. It doesn't matter. It doesn't matter. It doesn't matter. However much I try to repeat this mantra, I can't help wanting her to be the best – which is what we all want, surely, whether we use flashcards or not. If I ever hear anybody saying 'I don't mind if he's not academically gifted as long as he's happy' I just assume that they are lying – even to themselves. Short of being landed with a child prodigy, which can cause all sorts of other problems, we all want our kids to be good at things, and are ridiculously proud when they are. I'm just wary of crossing the line from justifiable parental pride and interest to unnecessary interference and overweening ambition.

When it comes to myself I am militantly uncompetitive and unambitious, but can't apply the same lackadaisical attitude to my child. I get ridiculously interested when she makes her regular announcements about what she wants to be when she grows up – as if it actually means anything. So far her ambitions have ranged from somebody who makes hot chocolate powder to 'a police' (she didn't specify man, woman, dog or horse). My wild suggestions are usually rejected out of hand. Medicine is a non-starter because she doesn't fancy the idea of anybody being sick over her, although she wouldn't mind being the sort of doctor she came to see with me, who just took my blood pressure, made a few jokes and tapped things into a computer. Writing is obviously out because she's seen what it does to her mother, who, at the risk of contracting rickets, often wastes a perfectly good sunny day by sitting at a keyboard for hours on end. (I'm doing it now.) Anything that involves performing in public – singing, dancing, acting – is dismissed out of hand because she doesn't really like doing things in front of an audience, although she did once toy with the idea of becoming an actress 'because I can do it on video'. While she's wittering on about the possibility of drawing pictures for a living (it has been done before) I'm envisaging glittering careers in the arts, science, music, accountancy – but it's all down to my vivid imagination and I'll just have to keep my dreams of glory to myself. People still laugh at me because I phoned everybody in my address book when the stabilisers came off her bike. In my defence I must say that she was only four and I thought it was a pretty damn fine achievement, but I recognised that my pride was just a whisker away from unhealthy gloating when other mothers whose children hadn't yet mastered two-wheelers were suitably impressed.

On the whole, though, my innate laziness will ultimately save me from turning into a fiercely competitive mother. I can't help my private thoughts and dreams, but I'd probably be horrified if I ended up having to sew three thousand sequins on a ball gown, or ferry her round to ice-skating rinks at five in the morning, or chess competitions or violin recitals. I'd love her to be talented at something, but not to the extent of actually having to do anything about it myself.

But I'm getting ahead of myself. Before I could start the daydreaming stage, and ponder the merits of a Pulitzer over an Oscar, she had quite a lot to do. Such as learning to walk and talk and smile without dribbling. My previously unknown competitive streak was probably born about the same time as she was, as the first few years seem to be just a series of tiny achievements that have to be ticked off in strict chronological order. While, of course, keeping a tally against other babies the same age. She can roll (tick), smile (tick), sit up (tick), stick her finger in her eye (tick). At this stage milestones are passed in rapid succession and each one is ridiculously exciting. I used to pore over the little book the health visitor gave me, gagging to add another attainment to the list. So why did I even bother to compare her to other babies if she was doing fine? What did it matter if Jack took his first steps three weeks earlier than she did, or Amy was positively dextrous with a spoon while my daughter was still at the flicking and smearing stage? Why did I indulge in all these completely pointless comparisons? Why did I rise to the bait of other mothers' blatant boasting? I even felt triumphant and reported it to bored friends and relations when she kicked a ball or got into a chair unaided. Why? Why? Why? Because I just couldn't help myself. I couldn't stop metaphorically peering into other people's potties. On the surface I thought I was quite relaxed about it all, quite sensible, but I kept on giving those sidelong glances at other babies and making mental calculations, while hating myself for doing it.

I came to the conclusion that however logical and sensible you are, there must be some sort of brain mechanism that mothers are wired up to, in order to alert them to any potential problems. If you think your baby is lovely, it might not occur to you that he should be able to walk by now, unless you see all his friends doing it. It's a bit of a lame theory, but the only explanation I can give for the mental torture I put myself through. While the sane half of my brain was assuring me that everything was fine and she was progressing normally, the mad-mother half was constantly whispering, 'She can't do that. Isn't he two weeks younger than her? Shouldn't her speech be clearer by now? Why does she keep falling over like that?' Sane mother enjoyed watching her acquire more and more life skills. Mad mother invented problems where there were none. 'Have you noticed,' I once remarked casually to her father, while secretly riffling through the Yellow Pages trying to find 'Linguistics, Professors of', 'that she doesn't say "spoon", she says "psoon". She always transposes the letters. There must be a name for that.' 'Yes,' he replied rather testily. 'Spoonerism.' I carefully returned the Yellow Pages to the shelf. Sane mother prevailed on that occasion, but mad mother was just retreating in order to regroup.

Mad mother would sometimes spring into action just when my guard was down. I'd be busily banging on to a friend about the difficulties of bedtimes, or mealtimes, or playtimes when I would suddenly realise that she was not agreeing with me. She wasn't making the required Sybil Fawlty squawkings of 'Oh I know, I *know*' and her children obviously didn't have any such problems. Sane mother shrugged it off and even – just for a nanosecond – considered asking advice. Mad mother either veered manically on to another subject or started flailing around trying to find some other example of my child's talents with which her children could not possibly compete. Sane and mad mothers combined forces to look down their noses at me for being such a prat.

Of course my daughter never knew she was being used as a yardstick and sailed through life perfectly normally, doing all the right things at the right times and fitting in perfectly well with her peer group. I didn't have much to worry about as far as she was concerned so I started worrying about myself. Will I never learn?

Before our daughter started her reception class we were invited to a parents' evening to learn about the school and what she would be doing there. It was an important occasion, so I sat there not listening to a word the teacher was saying because I was too busy looking round the room, pricing clothes, identifying potential friends, making mental notes of who to avoid at all costs and wondering how I would fit in to this motley crew of parents. There's always one in every class who nobody likes and I didn't want it to be me. This lot all (with a few terrifying exceptions) looked as if they'd read all the Ofsted reports and would be immediately signing up for the PTA and running the school fête and taking extra reading classes. But I was working! How would I find the time to throw myself into school life? Admittedly, even when I was a full-time housewife and mother I was never particularly good at bonding with mothers who weren't already friends of mine. I had an awful moment once, when joining a herd of buggies making for a toddlers' 'rhythm and movement' session in the park I fell into step with another mother I recognised vaguely from the playcentre. I wasn't actually looking forward to an afternoon of nursery rhymes and uncoordinated 'dancing' in a tent, so I happened to remark (perhaps a mite too caustically) 'For this I got an education.' I was rewarded with a tight little smile and she immediately accelerated, leaving us dawdling behind on the path. When I got to the tent I realised with horror that she was one of those professional mothers who was leading the singing. Oh shit. With one remark I had belittled her whole life's work. I felt really bad about it, but was a little heartened by the truly appalling behaviour of her own daughter. Actually the truth is, I wasn't a little heartened, I was completely elated. Her life's work obviously wasn't going too well.

Anyway, my life's work as I sat in that school hall was now divided between motherhood and paid employment. But just because I wouldn't be at home all the time I didn't want to be one of those absent mothers who can never remember the teacher's name. I wanted to be an accepted member of the mother-of-brat pack. After more staring around the room I hit on something that would be guaranteed to make me fit in. Blue toenails. They all had blue toenails. Well, if it was just a question of buying a bottle of Rimmel it was a jolly good start. Imagine the *faux pas* I could have made if I'd turned up on the first day of school with dusky pink peeping from my sandals.

With these ridiculous thoughts floating around my head I realised that most of what the teacher had been saying had not sunk in at all and it was time for a tour of the classrooms. Feeling an utter fraud I trooped off behind the others (will they be my friends?) and shuffled about a brightly painted room, fingering artwork that fell to bits and banging my shins on the child-sized furniture. All the intelligent questions I had prepared evaporated suddenly, but there was one woman who wasn't going to take anything on trust. She fixed on that teacher like a terrier, firing off questions about Ofsted and teacher–pupil ratios and literacy hours until I wanted to bite her. She certainly wasn't going to be my friend. Blistering bloody swot. Funnily enough I've never seen her again. Clearly all the things that I was quite impressed with didn't come up to her exacting standards and I expect she whisked her kid off to private school. I was content with the local primary, but still a bit concerned that it wouldn't be content with me.

(I did eventually make friends with one of the mothers but it probably had less to do with the school and more to do with the fact that we kept on bumping into each other browsing in the Beers, Wines and Spirits section of Sainsbury's. A shared interest is always a good basis for a friendship.)

So I joined the other mothers with a sense of trepidation. How was I going to measure up against them? My niece has a theory that if she takes her children to school when her hair's still wet it makes her look like a bad mother (disorganised slugabed). I was astonished at this. If I ever go to school with dry hair it's because I haven't had a shower at all and still have my pyjamas on under my clothes. It was also something that I hadn't thought of. Does it make me look like a disorganised slugabed? With a chance remark my niece had helpfully given me something else to worry about. How do I compare to others on the school run? Does anybody notice that I look a lot cleaner at 3p.m. than I do at 9a.m.? Why does Polly's mother, who I know for a fact doesn't work at all, turn up elegantly coiffed, in full slap and wearing fashionable clothes? Why does she bother? Why don't I bother? *Should* I bother? I decided to try bothering, but all that happened was that neighbours noticed I was wearing lipstick and started making jokes about me going to see my fancy man. That's why I don't bother. I think I suffer from a subconscious belief that mothers aren't really supposed to look glamorous. Clean, yes. Relatively alert, yes. But fiddling about with lip-brushes and earrings takes time – time that could be better spent either lying in bed for a few minutes longer or packing a nutritionally balanced lunchbox. This was one area in which I wasn't even going to attempt to compete; I allied myself firmly to the jeans and no makeup camp. I have to say that we are a lot more numerous than the lipsticked lot. We may be scruffy but we are legion.

So I fit in pretty well with the vast majority of the mothers at school in terms of mums' fashion stakes. However, other mothers who are also strangers to the mascara wand on school days have other ways of making me feel inadequate. I can't be the only one whose heart sinks when the words 'fancy dress' and 'school fête' are mentioned, but some mothers seem to positively relish the challenge. I admit defeat in the face of clever people who are constantly running up things on the sewing machine or creating junior flower gardens. The first time I was required to make a hat I was totally stumped. We managed it in the end and it was a good hat, it just wouldn't stay on her head. Why on earth should I be expected to make a hat? The midwife certainly never mentioned that it would be part of my duties. And even though we have piles of dressing-up clothes, when the school comes up with a 'beach party' theme for the fête, I haven't got a thing that's vaguely relevant, short of sending her to a chilly playground in a swimsuit and flip-flops. We dispensed with fancy dress on that occasion, but as I was queuing up for the surf simulator I noticed a couple of little girls running around in grass skirts and leis. That's forward thinking for you, but too late for me now, because if I start stocking the dressing-up box with Hawaiian shirts the next theme for the fête is bound to be 'Life with the Tudors'.

These constant demands on my resourcefulness can get a little trying. When our daughter was needed as a tree in the Christmas concert I got a note from the school telling me that all she would require for her costume would be a pair of brown trousers. Brown trousers? How many four-year-old girls do you know with brown trousers in their wardrobes? Couldn't she wear black tights and go as a burnt stick? I never did find any brown trousers, but I don't think it was because the rest of her class had cornered the market. I don't know what went on in that dressing room, but in the event all the 'trees' trooped on as lantern carriers in grey skirts – which is what they wear for school anyway. Brown trousers, indeed.

Christmas isn't too bad because they seem to make a lot of the required decorations and 'costumes' themselves (and why do they always make those crêpe paper crowns ever so slightly too big, thus ruining the close-ups on the video?), but my pathetic contributions to the school fête usually amount to no more than turning up on the day and spending money. Those jolly notices from school reminding us that the home-made cake stall is always very popular simply confirm my status as incompetent. One September I was determined to help out with something I *could* do, and carefully potted up dozens of cuttings that would be in full and glorious bloom for the following summer's fête. I'd show them! Then I forgot all about them, left them outside and lost the lot in the first frost of the year. Luckily I hadn't told anybody about my grandiose idea, so I fell back on Plan A and just turned up and spent money, handing it over rather shamefacedly to mothers whose talents in cake-baking, doll-making and mural-painting seemed to know no end.

I can't sing, can't dance – what can I do? Being able to recite limericks of dubious taste doesn't count for much with the PTA, and even though my talented ear for Anglo-Saxon came in very handy in my first-year exams at university, there isn't a lot of call for *Beowulf* on a day-to-day basis. Even her dad has a special skill. Our daughter once told him he was the best dad in the world 'because you can burp whenever I ask you to'. Again, not much use as a fund-raiser, but at least it's something. My creations will never feature on the home-made cake stall and, after a brief mental struggle, I have come to terms with that. However, being forced to use what's left of my imagination has occasionally produced some rather pleasing results. Last year's Easter bonnet was a *triumph*.

There's absolutely no point in trying to compete. I know that, and instead of beating myself up about it, I merely allow myself flashes of envy for other children's musical talents or other people's dressmaking skills. I'll never be able to run up a curtain and that's that. If I'm ever feeling particularly inadequate as a parent, however, I employ a simple yet effective cheer-up ruse. I take my daughter to Pizza Hut on the high street and secure a window table. While she scribbles with crayons and drops pizza in her lap I will sit with a glass of extremely ordinary wine and watch the world go by. This doesn't work with smart little pavement cafés in Soho, but I imagine that any bog-standard high street in the country will have the same effect. It doesn't take long before the passing outfits, hairstyles, slouching gaits and obvious gene deficiencies make me feel better about myself. Positively chipper, in fact. I might not look perfectly elegant when taking my daughter to school, but at least I don't look like an extra from *Deliverance*.

So if ever I find myself falling into the trap of making comparisons, I choose very carefully to whom I compare myself. And the same goes for her. If ever she irritates or annoys me, I only have to glance out of the window to be instantly grateful that at least she's not as dreadful as any of *that* bunch of misfits.

Chapter Ten

It's different when it's your own

I DON'T HAVE TO TRAVEL EVEN AS FAR AS Pizza Hut in order to size up the opposition. There are comparisons to be made much closer to home, and when my daughter is under scrutiny she often comes off pretty well. She and I enjoy a normal relationship with the right ratio of fun and fights. If she annoys me I tell her so, and she certainly isn't slow to criticise me if I do something wrong. For example, we often enjoy the following exchange:

'Mummy, will you take my shoes off?'

'I'm not wearing them.'

'You always say that!'

'Sorry.'

I regard it as a simple introduction to the joys of the English language; she sees it as a constant irritation. I haven't explained to her that an important part of any parent's job is to repeat weak jokes *ad nauseam* and embarrass their children. I'm just training her for my dotage. But on the whole we rub along pretty well. It's other children I sometimes have a problem with.

I freely admit that I'm not one of those women who loves to be surrounded by children. I think of them much as I would if they were people: some are tolerable; some are a positive pleasure to spend time with and some are to be avoided at all costs. And I'm not much good with babies, either. Despite having done a fair amount of baby-holding myself, when presented with somebody else's drooling bundle it doesn't ever give me the same feeling. I'm not proud of it, but whenever a new mother says to me, 'Would you like to hold him/her?' I have to fight the urge to say 'What for?' When my daughter was tiny I'm sure people must have thought I was terribly over-protective because instead of sensibly handing her over to all and sundry I had to wait to be asked. It simply didn't occur to me that people might actually *want* to risk being sicked on just for the chance to cuddle somebody else's baby. There, the truth is out. I absolutely adored having a baby only because she was my own. Tiny babies don't do much for me – they get much more interesting as they get older.

That's 'interesting' in the sense of the Chinese curse 'May you live in interesting times.' God knows it's difficult enough trying to 'read' a baby who does everything by instinct and can't communicate its wants and needs with anything more sophisticated than a loud yell. It's worse trying to reason with a toddler who also has wants and needs but who also doesn't seem to have progressed much beyond the loud yell. I could cope with my own because I knew her, and also, within the confines of the family, I was allowed to yell back. Yelling at other people's children, no matter how richly they may deserve it, seems to be rather frowned upon.

When my girl was a toddler, apart from a few massively public tantrums, she was generally quite quiet and reserved (that's all changed now, of course). When people remarked on her good behaviour I had to admit it was nothing to do with me. I hadn't moulded her manners, she was just like that. How nice, you might think, to have a naturally polite child. It might be, if they were all the same – but they're not, are they? It was a scene I had to endure countless times and I never really handled it properly. She would be sitting in the sandpit, happily playing with one of the toys provided by the playcentre, when another child would shamble over and wrest the toy from her grasp, sometimes with considerable force. Technically, this was a public toy to be used by everyone, but the unwritten rule was that you had to wait for another child to finish with a toy before appropriating it. Toddlers are not too hot on unwritten rules, though. Deprived of her plaything, and not being the type to just grab it back (or even hold on to it a bit tighter) my daughter would naturally look to me as her protector to do something about it. 'No, dear, give it back, she was playing with it' just never worked. The child would give me a toddler-type glare that conveyed the message 'Over my dead body, you interfering old bag.' I tried to glare back: 'Oh yeah? Well, that could be arranged,' but the child consistently refused to read my mind. What was I to do? Wrestling a three-year-old to the ground and administering the Vulcan death grip so it dropped the toy was a tempting thought, but not really an option. Muttering vicious threats would only cause the child to run screaming to its mother about the bad lady in the sandpit who was threatening violence. How firm was I allowed to be with unknown children? If the mother was nearby she would usually do the wrestling herself, hand back the toy apologetically then deal with her own toddler who was by now apoplectic with rage at having to give up some plastic bloody spade. Which, of course, made me feel guilty for having caused such upset because my daughter was incapable of coping with the jungle law of the playground. Plus, she obviously took a pretty dim view of my abilities as a protector. I failed on all counts.

When I wasn't involved in life-and-death struggles in the sand, I took time to study the other kids carefully. A lot of them would play happily enough in the sandpit, but only when tricked out in their favourite must-have outfits including jewellery and stick-on tattoos. The girls were even worse. Playgrounds, once ringing with the sounds of childish laughter and nursery rhymes (OK, with the odd maiming and torture as well) had turned into daylight night-clubs. The boys slouched and swaggered and appeared to be under the impression that Ali G is a serious fashion icon. And the girls! I thought it was a tad unusual the first time a five-year-old caused me to draw a sharp breath and murmur 'Jailbait'. Then it started happening all the time. Many of these prancing, posturing, preening, pouting little baggages with their wheedling and hair-flicking and bitchy little remarks could have given Jezebel a run for her money. Lolita was at least twelve before Humbert Humbert clapped eyes on her – well over the hill by today's standards. Where were the Peter Pan collars and ankle socks? When I at last spotted a hand-knitted jumper I think I did a double-take. The little boy who was wearing it, running about amid the sheepskin jackets (age 2–3), sequined T-shirts and cut-down catwalk ensembles looked as if he had just stepped out of the 1950s. I rather admired his mother for cocking a snook at prevailing fashions, but I wondered how long it would be before he noticed that he didn't look like the other boys and started demanding gold jewellery and shades.

With the example of other children constantly before her it's a struggle to bring up my daughter as a responsible and sensible citizen who wears proper clothes and doesn't spit in the street. Although God forbid she should become a prig, either...

To think I used to worry about her not mixing enough with other kids! More recently it has crossed my mind that it might be easier to bring her up on a remote island and teach her at home, just so I wouldn't have to cope with other children. I've lost count of the number of times I've heard the complaint, 'I don't know where he picks these things up. He was never like this before he went to school.' So I'm resigned to the fact that I have very little control over her social milieu or how she chooses her friends.

She made her first real friend when she was about two, but it was a rocky relationship. Joe lived a few doors away and was the same age, so they played together all the time, but I think it was a friendship based on proximity rather than a true meeting of minds. Gender was the least of their differences – chalk and cheese wasn't in it. I used to take them to the playgroup sometimes, firmly strapped into a double buggy, and they kept up a running commentary on objects of interest during the journey. 'Daffodils!' 'Digger!' 'Trees!' 'Truck!' Guess who said what. They were like boy and girl caricatures: sugar and spice meets slugs and snails and puppy dogs' tails. One day they were walking home and my girl found a snail on the pavement. She squatted down to have a look and Joe immediately ran up and stamped on it. This made her cry – a regular occurrence when Joe was around. They'd start off playing nicely then he'd pull her hair, push her over or pinch her and she'd start bawling. His mother tried to encourage her to stand up for herself while I tried to encourage her not to behave like Joe in any way, so there were some pretty mixed messages flying around. And yet they still clamoured to play with each other every day – God knows why. Eventually, though, the worm turned (I shouldn't really refer to my daughter as a worm, should I?) but unfortunately his mother wasn't there to witness it.

Joe was splashing me with water from the paddling pool, which I wasn't particularly bothered about, but it was whipping my daughter up into a fury. 'Stop doing that to my mummy!' she kept shouting, which of course made him do it even more until she finally lost it and walloped him. I was so shocked at this uncharacteristic behaviour that I cried out – so she burst into tears. She had been sorely provoked, but I suddenly found myself in the invidious position of telling my daughter that it was OK that she had just hit another child. What was I saying? At three years old there shouldn't be any grey areas – you don't hit other children and that's that. But because he had been such a pain I was actually quite sympathetic to her outburst, especially as she'd done it in my defence. Although I could hardly change the rule to: 'You must never ever hit another child, unless he's really asking for it', now could I? His mother's reaction when I told her was a gruff 'Good for her', but although I secretly agreed with her I was at a bit of a loss as to how to put things right with my daughter. And I was very cross with Joe. After all, if he did as he was told instead of acting like a hooligan then I wouldn't have had this problem in the first place. Bloody kids.

Joe was hard work, to put it mildly. They moved away eventually and I often wonder whether my daughter gained anything from constant exposure to such bad behaviour. Did she work out that if she copied him she would just get yelled at as much as he did? Probably. Did she take a silent vow never again to let a boy make her cry? I hope so. If they ever meet again she might find those karate lessons coming in handy. You see how illogical and inconsistent other children have made me? I naturally want my daughter to be studious and sensitive with an acute sense of social responsibility and a deep understanding of truth and beauty. She does karate merely in order to learn confidence, self-discipline and physical co-ordination, of course. But wouldn't I just love it if she put the fear of God into that pig-ignorant little monster who lives over the road. Kick ass, sweetie, but in a *good* way.

Since Joe, my daughter has moved on to a much wider

and more sophisticated circle of friends, and to my knowledge has never biffed any of them. I've come pretty close,
though. Her schoolfriends seem a pretty nice bunch, and
Joe must have had some effect on her because she appears
to have developed a marked aversion to 'naughty boys'.
(Let's hope that lasts into teenagehood.) They do normal
things: play games, give each other pictures and stickers, go
to each others' parties and haven't yet reached the stage of
swapping best friends, switching allegiances and generally
being unpleasant little bitches. I dare say that will come in
time, but so far her classmates have posed no problems.
There was one friend, though, who I thought seemed like a
nice little girl as she was always smiling. It was only when
I got to know her a bit better that I decided that her happy
face was a mask for a brain of startling inanity. Of course,
at five years old they are going to be skipping and singing
together, not analysing James Joyce, so I squashed my
snobby feelings because she is a nice little girl – even if she
did claim her father was David Beckham. Besides which, like
most parents, I have a very hazy idea of what goes on at
school, and I have absolutely no influence on my daughter's
choice of playmates, anyway. In vain I might suggest 'Why
don't you invite Laurie to your party, he seems like a nice
boy?' when what I really mean is that I quite like his mum.
If Laurie is 'too noisy' (which is rich coming from a girl who
has a nice line in high-pitched squealing) he gets crossed off

the invitation list. But such fine discrimination goes out of the window when it comes to the less controlled environment of the public playground.

Like any good middle-class mother I want my daughter only to play with 'naice' children. I don't want her picking up bad language, bad habits or bad behaviour. But she doesn't have her mother's radar for dodgy types and I can hardly say to her, 'Why don't I want you to play with Jade? Well, it's because she's eight years old and she already looks like a whore. Trust me on this one, she wouldn't be a good influence on you.' 'What's "whore", Mummy? And what does "influence" mean?' That's a very good question. How much 'influence' can another child really have? Unless Jade actually does something to positively upset my girl she will accept her blithely as a 'friend', and ignore all my dark mutterings about hidden agendas and manipulative little tarts. I should be grateful that my daughter is still so innocent and uncalculating, instead of worrying that she doesn't share my prejudices. Her father said to me the other day, about an old (an extremely old) schoolfriend, 'God, that man's a fool. No wonder my mother never liked me being his friend when we were kids' and I was reminded of my own mother's misgivings about Gary across the road. He was just the sort of boy who strikes fear into the heart of every mother in the neighbourhood: he was the archetypal 'bad influence'. My mother probably assumed that if I even spoke to him I would either be pregnant or hot-wiring cars by the time I was twelve. I had no such intentions, of course, but I bet it gave her a few bad moments when I decided that he was to be my buddy for the day.

And now I'm exactly the same with my own daughter. I conveniently forget that home life and parental influence actually do count for something, and start worrying frantically that some foul-mouthed eight-year-old is going to become her role model for life. So I'm constantly on the prowl, noting down examples of bad behaviour in order to incorporate them into long and boring parental lectures on the inadvisability of spitting, swearing, dropping litter or body piercing. With so many older children around it's got a bit beyond the toy-grabbing stage, and my daughter is often totally oblivious to the sort of behaviour that drives me, in a towering rage, into banishing all children from the house.

My own daughter, needless to say, is innocent and charming and reasonably well behaved. Other children are manipulative, rude and cunning – but they can't fool me. I know what children are really like: they are poisonous little wretches. If I was surrounded by happy, charming, polite children who played happily together and always said 'please' and 'thank you' I might feel differently about them. Luckily, I know enough children who are decent human beings to quell my King Herod tendencies, but on a bad day my thoughts are distinctly murderous.

Included in the incredibly long list of things that irritate me (wire coat hangers, chewing gum on the pavement, loud car horns, rucksacks on the tube, plastic cracker novelties and so on and so on) are TV police dramas. Not in their entirety, just the scene where a couple of burly coppers in macs go into somebody's sitting room and start picking up objects (usually framed photos) and examining them. They always do it and I always start shouting at the screen, 'Don't *do* that! You're in somebody else's house! Put it *down*!' The TV policemen don't listen to me and neither do the children who come into my house and behave in exactly the same way. Have they never been taught any manners at all? Diving into a toybox I can understand, but the little tykes who stroll in through the front door and start fingering my possessions are very lucky they've still got digits to finger with. Sometimes I feel as if I'm surrounded by children who were the models for Sid in *Toy Story*. Time to get something off my chest: 'My name is Kate and I don't like children very much.' They are nasty, brutish and short. I have a deep mistrust of anybody who claims to 'love kids'. You simply can't have an unqualified love of all children when so many of them are so unspeakably awful. When I see a group of children gathered together I react much as if I would if I suddenly came upon a lepers' convention. I turn sharply on my heel and walk briskly away. They're bound to be up to no good sooner or later and I'd rather not be there when it happens. Half a bottle of wine and a captive audience and I'll probably start sounding off about bringing back National Service. For ten-year-olds.

Naturally, it is different when it's your own. No doubt while I am looking with fond indulgence on my own daughter's little peccadilloes there will be some other adult in the room fuming with rage against the ill-mannered little madam. But I really believe I have just cause for my own fuming. In some ways I haven't progressed much beyond the toddler in the sandpit stage – I still don't know how to handle other kids' bad behaviour, and have on occasions found myself being incredibly sarcastic to a four-year-old who hasn't a clue what I'm on about, just to relieve my feelings. I also struggle with nature over nurture. I am, needless to say, a nice, well-brought-up, educated middle-class woman. I am also a rather bad-tempered Essex girl, and as they say, you can take the girl out of Essex... So my natural inclination, when faced with a nasty little brat, is not to say 'No, dear, don't do that', it is to boot the little bugger into the middle of next week. Having to squash my natural inclinations just makes me more bad-tempered.

Another of my problems, which is peculiar to my situation, is geography. We live in a cul-de-sac slap bang opposite a playground – which seemed like a good idea when she was one year old. As the years have passed and we've got to know some of the children who 'play' there I wonder whether it was such a good move. I have stood in that playground and watched my daughter and a bunch of girls happily playing 'What's the time Mr Wolf?' while a few yards away footballs and obscenities were flying around like bullets. Should I force my daughter to be the only child in the street who is not allowed to play outside? Of course not. She needs to mix with other children, learn how to socialise, how to hold her own against the older kids, how to be streetwise. But although I don't want to bring up a child like Little Lord Fauntleroy, I don't want Dennis the Menace either. It's a difficult tightrope to walk. I want my daughter to have friends, but not ones that I don't like. I only want her to have good influences, not bad ones. I want her neighbourhood chums to be able to distinguish between the playground and *my bloody house*. If I don't stand sentinel some kids are perfectly capable of just marching in (then picking things up and looking at them) as if they owned the place and it's taken ages to convince my daughter that children are like vampires: they are not allowed to cross the threshold unless they are invited. (I can think of a lot of other similarities as well, not least of which is that round here they seem to be a lot more active after dark.) My husband is much more benign than I am, maintaining that they're only kids and often it's not their fault if some of them don't see the world as I do. This was brought home to him one day when he was coming home and a small boy demanded:

'Whose house is this?'

'It's mine.'

'Where's your mum?'

'Well, she's dead.'

'Who killed her?'

I'm much less forgiving than my husband is, and if I catch him doling out biscuits to the locals hanging around the front door I start whispering fiercely: 'Don't encourage them! They're like stray animals – once they get a whiff of free food you'll never get rid of them!' and hope to God that my daughter doesn't get the idea that it's OK to go round to somebody else's house and say 'Got any chocolate?'

Oh, all right, I admit it. Children can be sweet and funny and my daughter has lots of fun just doing kids' stuff with other kids – riding bikes and getting dizzy on the roundabout and playing hopscotch. I like them to think that I'm a scary old dragon but they probably know that, for the ones I like, I'm just as much a soft touch as my husband. We're very lucky that our daughter can step outside her front door without getting mown down by a juggernaut, and that she can run around and not spend all her time in front of a

computer or TV screen. As a confirmed urbanite, it's
probably one of the best environments to grow up in that I
could wish for her. Fields and streams and open sky are
great for small children; they can look on all this beauty with
a rather jaundiced eye when they get to teenagehood. So she
is going to grow up in a city, rather than run away to one as
soon as she is able. But urban life can be a little rough
sometimes, so I have to be constantly aware of what she's
seeing and hearing and what ideas might be percolating in
her little brain. Claiming that your father is David Beckham
may be a tad extravagant, but not harmful. But short of
stopping her ears with cotton wool, I can't prevent some
pretty nasty stuff from getting through to her. I was horrified
when I found out that one little boy who lives nearby, let's
call him Sean, had told our au pair to fuck off. That's bad
enough, but my daughter's reaction, although basically
sound, contained one glaring error.

'Anyway, Sean's not my friend, I don't like him.'

'Good. I don't like him either.'

'And if I see him tomorrow and he's naughty again
   I'm going to tell *him* to fuck off.'

'Er, no, I think you're missing the point...'

Cue another long explanation and inward cursing of
other children and the problems they create for me that
wouldn't otherwise exist. Something I forgot to mention:

Sean is three years old, but he might not make it to four if our au pair has anything to do with it.

And so it goes on. My daughter has some perfectly nice playmates, but I'm tired of trying to explain to her that just because other children are still playing outside at nine o'clock at night doesn't mean that she can too. I'm tired of spending more time telling off other people's kids than I do my own. I'm tired of pointing out bad behaviour in others and wondering whether I'm warning her off it or just giving her ideas. I want *all* children to be good, and pleasant and malleable. I also want world peace and an end to floods and famine, which is probably more likely than the disappearance from the earth of all unpleasant children. So the lectures and the rages will continue while I continue to try to protect my daughter from some of the worst excesses of her peer group. There are occasions when that remote island still seems very appealing, but I have to tell myself that I cannot shield my daughter from all ugliness, and despite my misgivings about outside influences, it's highly unlikely that she will grow up into a juvenile delinquent with a mouth like a sewer. So when I think that bad children might be leading her astray I'll just tell them to fuck off, shall I?

Chapter Eleven

We never had videos, you know...

OF COURSE, THE SORT OF MONSTROUS BEHAVIOUR that I see around me now would never have happened in my day. We would never have been allowed the freedom and luxury that today's children enjoy. Don't know they're born, some of them. Having a child was a sure-fire way of setting me off thinking about my own childhood – the strict discipline, unheated bedrooms, porridge oats, rose-bay willowherb drifting across the desolate bomb sites that were our playgrounds...

Childhood has definitely changed since I had mine, which seems increasingly far away with every day that passes. (Note to self: that's because it is, stupid.) But initially I quite enjoyed trawling the memory banks for forgotten nursery rhymes and tunes, and made several phone calls to older siblings to see if they could remember what comes after 'Nebuchadnezzar, King of the Jews, bought his wife a pair of shoes...' It was huge fun singing '1, 2, 3, 4, 5 once I caught a fish alive...' except that it somehow put me in mind of Country Joe and the Fish and I found myself warbling 'Feel like I'm Fixing to Die'. It's a jolly tune to push a swing to, but I had to stop before she learned to talk. I could just imagine her being the only child in the playground trilling an anti-Vietnam war protest song and wondering why anybody would go home in a box not a buggy. Anyway, even though I was pleased to become reacquainted with some old favourites like 'Dance to your Daddy' I was obviously far too wrapped up in the past. I realised this when I was the only adult at the under-threes action songs and rhymes session mumbling into my chin because I'd never *heard* 'The wheels on the bus'. I've heard it a few times since, unfortunately. And then there was some utter bilge about sleeping bunnies which nearly finished me off before they launched into 'Here we go round the mulberry bush' and I felt on safer ground. 'It's OK, I know this one,' I assured my daughter, only to find that this fine old classic has been hijacked by some marketing executive for Ambre Solaire and we had to sing about putting on cream on a hot and sunny morning. I know, I know, it's terribly important, but really, is nothing sacred? What next? You shall have some Omega 5 on a little dishy?

Presumably we all started life as children, so in theory we should all know what it's like to be one – and sympathise. It was awful, wasn't it? Always having to do things you didn't want to, and not being able to do things you did want to, and life was really unfair. It wasn't helped by your mum always saying things like 'Because I said so,' and 'Not now, dear, Mummy's tired' and countless other banal phrases that you swore, with your little half-formed sense of justice, that you would never inflict on your own children (if any). I distinctly remember, at a very young age, wondering why my mother referred to herself in the third person. It seemed vaguely daft, but I couldn't explain it so just put it down to another of those mysteries that life is always throwing at you when you're little. My infant instincts were right, of course. It is vaguely daft, but I have since done it myself – and I still can't explain it. (I also have to own up to uttering that dread phrase 'You're not going out dressed like that' but would say in my defence that my daughter was very young at the time and proposing to parade the streets of London decked out in wellington boots, a straw hat and oven gloves. I promise I'll never say it again.)

Even if some of the words of nursery rhymes have crumbled to dust in my memory I'm sure I remember exactly what it was like to be a child. The injustices, the emotional traumas, the long periods of boredom and the infliction of totally unnecessary discipline. That's what childhood is all about, surely? Actually, it wasn't what my childhood was about and I hope it's not what my daughter's childhood is about either. I lied about the bomb sites. I remember the occasional traumas with a clarity that has hardly lessened over the years – as does every adult of my acquaintance – but I know now that my little crises were more likely to become the subjects of dinner party conversations about who had the most sadistic teachers, rather than the roots of deep neuroses. However, I know what it felt like at the time. Although I can't remove all pain and sadness from my daughter's life, I'd rather she didn't grow up with more than the average number of brooding resentments.

The latest crisis in her life came about because of a school assembly. You know the sort of thing: they take a theme and make up a little playlet about it. Usually she loves doing these and enters into the spirit of the thing with gusto, but when she brought home her 'script' she suddenly crumpled into tears and said she didn't want to do it. She didn't want to talk about it either, although it was clearly a matter of some importance to her. I was mystified, until I read her lines. She had been given the part of the naughty girl who doesn't listen, and obviously her problem was that she didn't want people to think that she was really like that. In vain we tried to convince her that it was only acting, and her teacher must think she was a really good actor if he gave her the part of the naughty girl, because everyone knew she was a good girl. She was genuinely upset and didn't want us to tell her teacher. So we did, of course, secretly, and he casually changed her part without letting her know that we had asked him to. She was like a puppy in that assembly, visibly fizzing with excitement and glee – a complete change from the miserable little girl who thought she had the weight of the world on her shoulders.

I was so glad we had sorted it out for her, but maybe we should have just made her do the assembly to teach her the valuable life lesson that sometimes you have to do things you don't want to. She'll have to get used to it after all, and it doesn't do to mollycoddle children. Life isn't fair, and the sooner they learn that the better. However, you can call me an old softie if you like, but when faced with a five-year-old who is genuinely upset about something my instinct is to try and make it better if I can. One of the criticisms of *Teletubbies* was that it presents a perfect world where nothing ever goes wrong and the world isn't like that. But it is aimed at two- to three-year-olds. I certainly don't want to start explaining war and poverty to a pre-schooler. If you ignore the more appropriate criticism of the programme that it's probably not a good idea to encourage such young children to watch the box in the first place, if she's going to watch TV I'd rather it was *Teletubbies* than *Titus Andronicus*. She'll have a life full of the pain and misery that plague us all at some time, so while she's young I want her, as far as possible, to be happy. On the whole, I was, and it never did me any harm. (Damn, one of those mumsy phrases just crept in again.) So I do my best to solve her problems and smooth out injustices and generally show her a good time. There's plenty of time to toughen her up – I give it another two weeks before I start showing her the ugly side of life.

It happened to me when I was about eight or nine. As a Christmas treat at school we were promised a showing of a *Just William* film. We were all terribly excited at the prospect of sitting cross-legged on a hard floor to watch an old black-and-white film with no special effects and a rather scratchy soundtrack. Then, when we were all gathered in the large hall, fidgeting and whispering, our form teacher came in and told us that he was sorry, but the projector was broken and we'd all have to return, in single file, to our classrooms to do our usual lessons. A mass sigh of disappointment filled the hall, but we trooped back as we had been told. Now, I may or may not have been a particularly suspicious child, but he didn't look too sorry to me, and the thought crossed my mind that this was a put-up job to teach us a hard lesson in life about how to cope with disappointment.

Christmas was just around the corner, after all. I never voiced my suspicions, and was too young to have heard of conspiracy theories, but to this day I remember the expression on his face which suggested to me, 'Serves you right you spoilt little blighters.'

Now, of course, the entire staff and board of governors would probably have leapt into action in order to compensate the spoilt little blighters for their mild disappointment. Maybe we were wrong to try to sort out our daughter's acting angst. I'm sure nobody would have gone to any trouble on my behalf if I had behaved with such appalling lack of backbone. Come to think of it, why am I bothering to smooth out her problems for her? Am I just encouraging her to become a spineless wimp? Kids today have no idea how indulged they are and will get into the most awful strops about the tiniest of setbacks. It's not as if they've got anything to be stroppy about. No exams, no acne, no disastrous love affairs, no hair in funny places, no responsibilities, no reason to do anything other than skip through life singing a happy song. Instead they just invent excuses for thinking the whole world is against them and nobody understands that making them clean their teeth just ISN'T FAIR! I seem to remember that when I was a kid there wasn't actually a choice about it, and I would have got into big trouble if I'd questioned the necessity of cleaning my teeth. I get terribly cross with my daughter sometimes and start hearing myself saying 'Why can't you just do as you're told? Why does there always have to be an argument about it?' I had fondly thought that, as a parent, when you gave instructions they would be followed. Commands would be obeyed with alacrity and no child of mine would ever answer back. A mere raised eyebrow would have her scuttling to clean her teeth or tidy her room while I congratulated myself on my excellent parenting skills. That's how I was brought up and she was going to be subject to the same discipline. Needless to say, it's not quite like that.

As a child one of my greatest causes of complaint was being forbidden to do things for no good reason, as far as I could see. So as a mother I made the mistake of always trying to find a reason for my bans, refusals and general unwillingness to join in tedious and messy games. 'Because I don't feel like it' always seemed like a rather lame excuse for not wanting to be bandaged or do a Tweenies jigsaw and as an adult I should be better able than my daughter to cope with disappointment, tiredness and boredom. What a fool I was. If I'd trained her when she was younger to accept a totally unjustified 'No you can't' without explanation, I wouldn't now have to give all those lectures about the nature of tube travel and how it doesn't really set you up too well for a vigorous game of badminton the second you walk through the front door. 'I've just cleaned that!' is now generally understood to be a general ban on muddy shoes, paper-cutting or doll-washing, but I wasted a lot of time trying to explain things when I should have just used that old standby 'Because you're not allowed to'. Although I didn't realise it at the time, it worked for me when I was a kid. Why did I have to over-complicate things?

So my attempt to smooth the path of life for my little girl has seriously backfired. It's my own fault if I mutter darkly about the vanished concept of 'seen and not heard'. It's gone the way of respecting your elders and betters, proper children's clothes, torches under the bedclothes and boys wanting to be train drivers, I suppose. Down the pan along with Muffin the Mule. Too late, too late. If I'd wanted to be strict I shouldn't have been so lazy. I wasn't being concerned and caring, I was being idle. It was more trouble to impose strict discipline than it was to just let her dig holes in the flowerbeds and fill them in later. Too indolent to spend my days saying 'Don't do that', I have to suffer the consequences, and can't really complain now if she gets a little argumentative when I say 'No'. At least she's well-behaved with other people. It's just her parents she treats like dirt. Better than the other way round, I suppose.

We've all heard the complaints. Childhood isn't childhood any more. They are made into mini-adults far too soon, bombarded with media images that make them into greedy little consumers even before they can lisp 'Three-year guarantee'. Lack of discipline, lack of respect, immense over-indulgence of their every whim – it was never like that in my day. It took me weeks to save the 4/11 it cost to get a ball on a string that you hooped round your ankle and jumped over. My daughter now expects me to shell out £14.99 for the latest Harry Potter video at the drop of a hat. What's gone wrong?

In our child-centred world I sometimes think that maybe she has too much of a good time. If I had a serene childhood without the aid of videos, Pizza Hut and Kinder toy collections, why can't she? I just can't stop the parental grumbling in the age-old vein of 'We never had...' and 'When I was your age...'. It goes in one ear and out the other, of course. When her father tells her that, not only did we not have videos, he didn't even have a television when he was a child, I can see that she doesn't really believe him. It's obviously a bit like me trying to imagine life without electricity or running water. Although we never had central heating, you know...

And why aren't children ever allowed to be bored? Surely it's the finest preparation for later life you can give them. How do I explain to my daughter about the importance of having inner resources? Perhaps I should teach her how to play solitaire, now we've mastered snakes and ladders, and point out that you don't actually have to have an audience to read a book. I haven't tried it yet, but I'm considering taking her somewhere where she has to stand

and look at things and think about them. No buttons to push or handles to turn, nothing to climb on or jump off or run around. Lots of glass cases full of artefacts from the distant past, dusty stuffed animals and bits of broken pottery. This was brought on when I was scanning the paper and thought 'Oh, good, Tate Modern does children's activities. Maybe I'll take her there.' This thought was swiftly followed by a massive rebellion: 'Oh sod it. Why does she need to be entertained all the time? We can go to the Wallace Collection. I like it and she can jolly well put up with it for the sake of seeing the Old Dutch Masters. It might make her grateful if she sees the sorts of clothes that children used to have to wear.' She'd probably last about fifteen minutes and I'd have to bribe her with the promise of pizza, but perhaps it's worth a try, because I'm heartily sick and tired of the Science Museum. I suspect also, despite all the helpers and explanatory notes and demonstrations of bubble-making, all this mucking about with buttons and handles teaches her bugger all about science. When I was a kid the most exciting thing there was a static electricity demonstration that made your hair stand on end. In the Natural History Museum, the dinosaurs were bones, not animatronics, and it didn't make them any less fascinating. The fact that they didn't move about or roar didn't put me off, and I treasured the odd postcard of a fossil. It didn't bother me that there wasn't a gift shop round every corner and I suspect my mother was pretty grateful as well. I don't think my daughter could cope with going to see anything that didn't have a shop attached to it, including farms, beaches and mountaintops, let alone museums. When I was a child our parents took us to Kimmeridge Bay and we spent a rather chilly afternoon looking for real fossils. My daughter comes away from the Natural History Museum, not with an imagination fired with a love of the natural world, but with a tube full of plastic dinosaurs. Spoilt rotten.

I'm thinking of starting a Campaign for Real Kids. One that will foster a breed of pre-war types who polish their own shoes, eat their greens, call their fathers Sir and whose most violent form of dissent is to beseech quietly, 'Oh, mayn't I, Mother, mayn't I?' What are its chances? Pretty slim, I suspect.

We can't help doing it – wondering, when you're dolloping out oven chips and calculating the spiralling cost of party bags, whose stupid bloody idea was it to put a prize in every layer of pass the parcel and how we never had this when we were kids. But even though we were never allowed to play in the street; eat between meals; have long hair; wear what we wanted; complain about being bored; bother grown-ups when they had other things to do; leave the table without asking permission, etc. etc. we will do things for our own children that our own parents would never have contemplated doing for us. But surely 'twas ever thus? Are we really being soft, or just trying to improve on the childhoods that we had (as surely all parents do)? Isn't it better that children no longer have to sit at inky desks learning by rote, or go up chimneys or wear uncomfortable clothes?

Do I really remember it that well? I know I wasn't allowed to misbehave. Or is it closer to the truth to say that I wasn't supposed to misbehave, but did anyway. I *imagine* I did as I was told, we all did. But when offered the encouragement of a couple of glasses of sherry my mother will launch happily into stories about my older siblings cutting each other's hair or making soup out of washing-up liquid and soap powder or smearing their faces and the floor with shoe polish. If I dig a little deeper into my memory I have to admit that I didn't actually spend my entire childhood dressed in Peter Pan collars and dresses with sashes, quietly reading *Swallows and Amazons*. I did a lot of things I knew I wasn't supposed to and sometimes I got away with it.

Still, even though I can't help muttering darkly about kids today not knowing they're born and how they have no respect and no manners, I suspect that things don't really change that much, it's just a question of degree. After all, well before lager was invented, around the streets of nineteenth-century London roamed gangs of hooligans bent on mischief of an extremely violent nature. And what about all the fuss that was made about that podgy little rebel, Bill Haley? Don't those panellists on *Any Questions* look a right bunch of idiots now?

Instead of trying to conjure up some golden era that never really existed perhaps I should try to be a little more honest with myself. For example, I loathe Kinder eggs with a passion, and am constantly shovelling bits of plastic into the bin and complaining about unnecessary junk. But children have always been acquisitive little magpies, whether they're collecting bits of fallen Spitfire or Pokémon cards. It's just stuff to them. We had 'diamonds' when I was a kid. Collections of sparkly stones and bits of broken jewellery that were terribly, terribly precious and excellent for 'swapsies'. It's those clever marketing people who have tapped into the fact that children love collecting things and what's the point of them getting all fired up about bus tickets and curiously shaped stones when you can sell them stuff instead? Spitfire bits were cheaper, but most parents would rather shell out the cash than put up with the attendant dangers of air raids and bomb sites. That's why it was sheer marketing genius to put a toy in a chocolate egg, and why our fridge is decorated with completely useless Kitecat magnets ('Collect all 10!' God, do we have to?). I expect I left 'diamonds' all over the house too, ready to be stepped on in bare feet or jam the Hoover mechanism.

Likewise I'm always complaining about the extent of my daughter's wardrobe and the truly hideous outfits that beckon to her from the clothes rails. I conveniently gloss over the fact that I was a teenager in the 70s – the decade that fashion forgot. I embraced flares, tank tops and cheese-cloth with the same passion as she now pounces on sparkly trousers and T-shirts emblazoned with stupid phrases such as 'Cool Chick'. I shudder, but it's her favourite. But let's face it, fashion has always been regarded with horror by people at whom it is not directed, otherwise there wouldn't be any point in it. Dressing five-year-old girls as streetwalkers is not and has never been a good idea, but I can usually find something my daughter likes and I can tolerate, without forcing her into the sensible brogues and pinafores that I favour. If I wanted her to look like a smart continental child I should never have given her a say in what she wears. When browsing for summer outfits, for example, I found a lovely pair of beige deck shoes that I tried to force on her. She chose pink sandals with flowers on them. I gave a deep sigh and allowed her to have the sandals. I now do things I swore I never would, like buying clothes for her that I don't like, simply because she's a little girl and I know she would prefer a T-shirt with glittery hearts on it to the plain navy number that I had my eye on. I look forward to the day when she finally appreciates the joy of a well-cut black jacket unadorned with sequins or flowers, but until then I shall just close my eyes to all the various shades of pink that fill her wardrobe, just the way my mother didn't complain (that) much about my black eyeshadow and platform boots.

And although, among my other clichéd parental statements, I might complain that I don't know what they teach them in schools nowadays, it wasn't exactly Dotheboys Hall at my school, if I'm honest. We didn't all sit in silent rows doing sums, and we weren't all perfectly well behaved. There was a particular child in my infant school who was completely out of control. Our teacher (whom I remember as being called Miss Dungeon, but I may have got that wrong) used to get big red blotches on her neck when Adam started creating merry hell, and even in those distant days I'm sure he wasn't the first kid in the world to be an undisciplined hooligan.

Of course our parents thought exactly the same about our privileged, feather-bedded childhoods when we knew no want. Children have no opinions on it. They just accept what's there. You don't catch them thinking 'Wow! A video recorder! Computer games! How lucky am I to have been born into such an advanced technological age!' I can't turn the clock back to liberty bodices and paraffin oil heaters and nor would I want to. My older siblings have probably never forgiven me for the fact that by the time I was old enough to swallow solid food, cod liver oil capsules had been replaced by the much more palatable Haliborange tablets, but that was just my sheer good luck. The lives of children have improved in lots of ways. I had Harry Worth once a week in black and white and she has *Shrek* on video. I had to stay at home for the first five years of my life before being suddenly slung into a full day of school five days a week. She had playgroup, nursery and reception to ease her gradually into the world of academia. I know which I'd prefer. (*Shrek*, obviously.) There always have been, and always will be, spoilt brats with too much money, too much parental indulgence and not enough discipline. I hope my daughter is not one of them, but I'm not going to turn the central heating off just to prove a point.

Chapter Twelve

Different strokes for different folks

THINGS MAY OR MAY NOT HAVE CHANGED SINCE
my childhood, but people will still insist on having
children and bringing them up, and it's amazing the different ways they go about it. After a while I sort of settled into
my way of doing things, which I guess is what most parents
do, and it's only when you get a glimpse of other families
that you realise just how varied domestic set-ups can be.
Just look at any episode of *Rugrats* to get an idea of different parenting styles. You can be a domesticated homebody,
high-powered executive, wacky fun lover or (in the early
series before he remarried) diffident single dad, and still get
the job done.

Obviously there are constraints on every family. Time,
money, personal characteristics and the size of your home

play a large part in how you order your domestic life. I can't *choose* to be a strict disciplinarian with rules on every area of life, because I would simply forget what they were, have second thoughts and decide I couldn't be bothered to enforce them anyway. Likewise, the idea of travelling the world with my daughter and bringing her up with a wide experience of different places and cultures would have a lasting effect on her whole life, but the pressure of those two-pronged evils of time and money means that it's not going to happen. I sometimes think that the whole tenor of our lives would change (for the better) if we had a kitchen big enough to eat in. (Eat in while sitting down, I mean, not standing over the sink dropping sandwich crumbs down the plughole.) So you can't always – no, you can't *ever* – make a blueprint of how you are going to run your life and stick to it. Too many external factors, whether it's the size of the second bedroom or what time you get home from work, will conspire against your well-laid plans and force you to work around the circumstances that life has given you. And within these constraints there are more different routes to follow than in the London A to Z.

But the way in which other people run their lives is a constant source of fascination to me. This absorption probably started when I was a kid and I mentioned to a schoolfriend that now my sister was going out to work she was paying rent to my mother. My schoolfriend was horrified that my mother should accept money from her own daughter; I was horrified that in their family it was acceptable to take free board and lodging from people who had been paying through the nose for you for your entire life. Since then, other people's domestic habits have remained for me far more interesting than their sexual peccadilloes. I don't care how many affairs you've had – how do you clean your toilet? The ways people choose to perform simple household tasks can be a real eye-opener. I chortled with glee, mixed with disbelief, when a friend told me that when she had American friends staying they expected her to change their sheets every day. 'Good grief,' she said, 'the sheets don't get changed in this house until they are turning brown.' I think she was exaggerating slightly, but even so, who on earth changes their sheets *every day*? American friends, obviously. On the same subject, we once had a long and engrossing conversation at work about morning bed-making habits.

'Of course I always make the bed properly before I leave the house. I couldn't come back to an unmade bed.'

'No, no, no. If you make it properly then it's not getting aired. It's not tidy, it's festering.'

'I think that's just an excuse for not making the bed.'

'No, you can turn the duvet back neatly and it
looks fine. Your bed must be smouldering with
night sweats and discarded skin cells.'

'Rubbish! My bed doesn't smoulder. I change the
sheets regularly. How often do you change
yours – or do you just leave it to "air"?'

This went on for some time, and nobody won the argument.
Bed-making is just one area that is ripe for heated dispute.
Washing up is another. I think it is positively insanitary to
use a washing-up bowl – running water only is the rule in
our house. My daughter has never lisped charmingly,
'Mummy, why are your hands so soft?' but it's not because
they are covered in a layer of grease and oil that has been
lying like scum on the surface of the water in the washing-
up bowl. Sorry. That's just one of my own little hobby-horses.
Another acquaintance would practically puke if you suggested using a brush for cleaning pots and pans: 'Yuk!
That's filthy!' Do you dry up or leave to drain? Do you
shower in the morning or bath at night? Do you think it's
OK to make five lots of sandwiches for the week and leave
them in the fridge in clingfilm, or do you make a fresh lot
every morning? How many times can you use a teabag? Do
you put a crease in shirt-sleeves? Such domestic minutiae
are, if discussed in public, minefields of disagreement, strife
and mutual disgust. Some people are positively perverse in

their domestic habits. Some people, for example, *put the milk in first*. Bizarre behaviour.

So if a squabble about whether or not you use a wooden chopping board can almost lead to fisticuffs, imagine the diverse opinions on how to bring up children. There are no British Standards for parenting, so most people just make it up as they go along, under the influence of their own experience and, to some extent, fashion.

At first it was those swings in fashion that confused me a little. Burp them; don't burp them; put them to sleep on their backs, their fronts, their sides, the floor, the ceiling; let them cry; never let them cry; potty-train them at six months; wait until they're eighteen and it's getting embarrassing; have proper mealtimes; let them graze; have the father at the birth; send him to the pub, he'll only get in the way – it just goes on and on. Even with a small baby, which you would think would require the same style of care from everybody, there are different schools of thought. People are still formulating different (yet always 'foolproof') methods of regulating sleep patterns, but at least we don't have to do four-hour feeds any more. Imagine deliberately waking up a peacefully sleeping baby in order to feed it. How mad was that? Not as mad as the baby, obviously, which was rudely awakened from a peaceful slumber by its exhausted mother, just for the pleasure of drinking some milk that was probably sicked up anyway.

But competing theories still abound, much to the disapproval of our own mothers who did it their way and it was the best way. I note that swaddling is back in favour, for example, which is a brilliant idea. I've got no idea what it does for babies, but I can think of countless five- to eight-year-olds who would benefit from a thoroughly efficient swaddle, the tighter the better (not to mention the attendant benefits to their families and surrounding districts).

Some fashions can be more abiding and more destructive than others. Remember the theories on progressive parenting? Letting children learn by expressing themselves? I can't imagine why this one had such a long run, unless it was a convenient excuse for not actually doing anything at all. Maybe there was a touch of the Emperor's New Clothes about it all: nobody wanted to look like an old-fashioned disciplinarian, so we put up with other people's children pursuing their development in our living rooms with all the subtlety of an invading army until the collective, pent-up roar of 'ENOUGH!'. I don't know why it took us all so long to admit it: rampaging kids with dippy parents are a pain in the bum, fully developed or not. A friend of mine claimed knowledge of a real lulu. She told me that she once gave a mild rebuke to a friend of hers with very strange ideas on discipline because she was allowing her son to play football in an art gallery. The reply this deranged mother gave was, 'He's appreciating art in his own way.' Much to her credit, my friend refrained from retorting 'I find the only way I can truly appreciate art is by simultaneously administering Chinese burns to a small child,' but she must have been tempted to sit him down in front of *Guernica* while uttering vague but menacing threats.

My father always used to joke: 'The aristocracy have got the right idea. They get their children brought up by nannies and then as soon as they are old enough they pack them off to boarding-school.' At least I think he was joking. It was probably a lifelong ambition of his to get us out from under his feet. As I recall, we were asked quite regularly when we were thinking of leaving home. His 'hands off' ideal of parenthood was deliberately extreme and probably intended as a not very subtle reminder to us to be a bit bloody quieter. But even he must have been forced to admit that it's a good thing that children no longer have to stay in the nursery all day, only seeing Mummy and Daddy (or 'Mater' and 'Pater') for five minutes after supper when they're allowed in the drawing room to receive a goodnight kiss. Imagine! You'd never see them at all! Never enjoy bathtimes or mealtimes or kicking a football around. Never get to nurse them through illness or coach them in table manners. How dreadful. Or how restful.

On second thoughts, I seem to be rather coming round to my father's point of view. When I'm begging '*Please* could you leave me alone for five minutes' the idea of long-distance parenthood seems mighty attractive. Some people seem to manage the twenty-first-century version of it quite well. You probably need more domestic staff than a small royal palace to re-create the same distance as a Victorian patriarch, but with the right complement of nannies, au pairs, childminders, cleaners, ironers, gardeners and social secretaries you could probably pay your way into the happy situation of only seeing your children when they have already been fed, washed, disciplined and entertained and you can just enjoy their company. Children as pets! It's an excellent idea – I know lots of pets that lead lives of pampered bliss and their owners never have to go to the bother of training or educating them.

All right, I have inherited my father's fondness for comic exaggeration, but even without going to such extremes you could argue that it might make you a calmer, more fulfilled and more pleasant mother if it isn't *always* you who has to clean up the sick. The ability to pay somebody else to do it once in a while probably means that you have paid employment yourself and so you are bound at some point to get sucked into the 'go to work/stay at home' argument which continues to rage. I don't know why we still bother to discuss it: each side claims higher moral ground than the other and everybody thinks they're hard done by. After all, 'I don't know how she does it' might equally apply to a woman who stays at home with a couple of pre-schoolers to look after all day long. And just when you think you've struck a happy balance some helpful academic does a bloody study on us and finds out that children thrive best when their mothers stay at home for six months/two years/half an hour before going back to work, but only until two o'clock in the afternoon on alternate Thursdays. Thank you. That makes everything clear. Has anybody been listening to me? Am I talking to myself? I repeat: whatever you do is wrong, so there's no point in arguing about it.

So don't talk to me about whether it's 'best' to stay at home with your children or to fulfil yourself in your working life. Quite apart from the fact that very few people have a genuine choice as to whether to work for something or for nothing, what's 'best' is what works for you and your family. I try very hard not to judge how other families choose to run their lives (what a complete lie) but some people are so peculiar it's difficult not to.

The arm's-length style of parenting remains a fond dream for me, just as it did for my father. Without the resources to fund such a lifestyle we both had to be a little more personally responsible for our offspring, but other methods are open to most people depending on their disposition. I have known some parents, overcome by the responsibility thrust upon them, who have tried to do everything by the book, literally, and instead of trusting their own instincts chose to rely on the word of 'experts'. Doctor

Spock had a really good run for his money before he went out of fashion, after all. I've never read his ideas on child-care, but if I had ever given it any thought, it might have struck me as odd that generations of children were being brought up according to the dictates of one man. Now there are hordes of pundits plying their theories, and I think it's fine to read books if you feel that you are getting much-needed help from professionals who know what they are talking about. However, I would run like the wind from anyone who is referred to as a 'guru'. I'm not sure exactly what it means, but I think it's something like 'unqualified but opinionated'. If I read any more guff about approaching life with a serene frame of mind, lifestyle priorities, incorporat-ing spirituality into everyday activities or becoming part of the wonder and excitement of childhood I may be forced to do something violent. What does it all mean? 'Try lighting a candle in the morning or listening to Mozart instead of the news.' Fuck *off*. You light a candle and I'll get the breakfast ready. These same people then have the nerve to tell you how important it is not to lose your sense of humour. Which is fine, because I'll feel better about laughing my head off while delivering a good hard slap.

Without having to light candles or breathe deeply, at least we are all a little more relaxed about life than in the days of four-hour feeds and newborn babies that could only be viewed from behind glass (which expert thought up that little wheeze, I wonder?). Thank God for that, although some parents can be more relaxed than others. I find it quite stressful to spend time with an over-anxious mother, who is constantly spraying everything with anti-bacterial liquid and cleaning the carpet with tweezers. I start to feel guilty about not wearing an anti-contamination suit and wondering whether I should really be allowing my daughter to walk about without full body armour, and I always leave such encounters feeling grubby and irresponsible. But, just as it is possible to be so open-minded that your brains fall out, you can also be so laid back that you fall on your bum. If I get fidgety in the company of an over-anxious mother, I get quietly hysterical when I think somebody's being a little *too* relaxed. I know we've all said it: 'There's no blood, it must be OK', but surely not in the face of visibly swelling contusions. And I know it doesn't do to interfere, but when I start casually putting knives away, separating fighting children and wiping off snot that I'm not related to, it's a sure sign that I'm thinking that somebody isn't doing their job properly. Being relaxed and laid back about parenting is a good idea up to a point, but not when you start using it as an excuse just to let them fend for themselves. The one advantage of being with these parents is that you have to do very little apologising for your own children, but it's a style I try not to adopt myself, and if I find myself being so easy-going that I suspect I'm just avoiding confrontation I will give myself a good talking-to. I don't always listen, of course, but hey, I can sort it out another time.

Even if I will admit to being myself at different times either over-anxious or over-relaxed, there's one type of mother I really can't abide. I'd shoot myself if I ever thought I was becoming a martyr. The perpetrator of the deep sigh and carefully staged self-sacrifice is a subject for my particular disdain. We've all had to struggle with childcare while suffering from a heavy cold, for example, but most of us prefer it if we have the chance to take to our beds instead. We don't regard illness as the perfect opportunity to look pained but heroic and battle on, spreading our germs throughout the neighbourhood in the process. Do these women think that other people admire them for their hard work and stoicism? Well, I don't; I am just irritated by them for letting the side down. Do they think their children appreciate their willingness to put them first at any expense? 'It's all right, darling, I'm sure the crutches won't interfere too much with me being in goal, if you *really* want to play three-and-in.' Well they don't, they just take her for a sucker and will probably grow up to be selfish and demanding and incapable of tying their own shoelaces. Martyr mothers are quite as offensive as scummy washing-up bowls, in my irritable opinion.

However (with that evil rant off my chest), even if your general overview of life may be broadly the same as that of your peers, in certain specific areas methods of parenting

can differ wildly. Take smacking. We don't do it. It is decidedly not our style, and although I might talk a lot (even
fantasise a lot) about administering a jolly good hiding,
I would never actually do it. I wasn't smacked as a child; my
husband was regularly thrashed, but we both came inde-
pendently to the same conclusion: it wasn't for us or for our
daughter. But other people come to different conclusions. I
knew one woman who was constantly walloping her little
boy. She maintained that he was so – how shall I put this –
'boisterous' that she'd tried everything else and it was the
only way to get through to him. Personally, I thought it
made him worse. At the other end of the scale I knew
another woman with a small boy who told me quite seriously that you should never show children that you are
angry. She was barking mad, of course, in a quiet, non-
aggressive sort of way, and her boy didn't seem to appreciate
her efforts. He could commit the most heinous crimes,
always to be met with the same calm, caring, careful explanations about how it wasn't really a good idea to tie the cat
to the banisters and he wouldn't do it again, would he?
Personally, I thought it made him worse. She was always
buying books on toddler taming, how to control your child,
how not to let your child walk all over you, how to apologise
to other people for your child's behaviour, the effective use
of a cattle prod in child-rearing and so on. I suppose she
read them, but she might have been better advised just to

chuck them at him. (See, I'm all talk.)

These two women represent opposite ends of the discipline spectrum, neither of which I thought particularly effective. I sneer at compulsive wallopers just as much as I do at those limp women with badly behaved children who are constantly murmuring 'Don't do that, darling' only to be totally ignored or possibly kicked. I'm somewhere in the middle. I shout quietly, I have absolutely no compunction about displaying temper, I lecture, I complain bitterly and I whine. 'Oh, what did you do *that* for? Now I'll have to do it all over again. It's just making more work for me, you know. Honestly, I just don't know why I bother, sometimes...' It's not pretty, but it gets the job done. I'm so unbearable when I'm whining that my daughter will do anything just to put a stop to the constant drone.

So what informs our decisions about what sort of parents we will be? What has made me into a whiner and my friend into a walloper? Our own childhood experiences, certainly, whether we try to reproduce them or reverse them for our own children. Vague or strongly held beliefs, probably. Other influences, social pressures, what we've been used to ourselves – or what other people think we ought to be used to.

Among all the real-life examples of other parents that surround us, there are also their fictional counterparts. I might snort with derision at the Oxo family, but they do have a kitchen big enough to eat in and it obviously has a profound effect on their life as a family. They look as though they are supposed to be everyone's idea of normality, and not just because they've got a big table. They're not perfect, but they're *better than us* – a nasty, insidious way of making us all feel a little bit worse about ourselves. Evidently I am more influenced by advertising than I think I am, and as I stare unthinkingly at clean kitchens, happy family meals, bright white shirts and sitting rooms with flowers in them, some of it is seeping into my brain and making me vaguely discontented. Is that what we're really supposed to be like? Are Mr and Mrs Oxo and women with shiny hair and fridges full of fruit yoghurt the benchmarks for all parents? God forbid.

But fictional families do have their influences for good or evil, as was *nearly* recognised by George Bush senior when he publicly wished that American families could be more like the Waltons and less like the Simpsons. It was a neat turn of phrase but a damnable slur on the Simpsons. I can't understand why they have this reputation as a dysfunctional family. They may get into the odd scrape (as do we all) but basically they love and support each other (as should we all). I wouldn't mind too much if my daughter turned out like Lisa Simpson (not the hair though). Perhaps not Bart, I admit, although even he has plenty of redeeming features (not the hair, though). I also seem to remember that it was a Walton, not a Simpson, who suggested hanging Father

Christmas up by the balls. And at least Marge seems to be a more caring mother than Deedee Pickles, who despite her well-thumbed copy of Lipschitz and her *apparent* love for Tommy and Dill, is constantly losing her own and other children and allowing them to get into situations of extraordinary danger. I'm surprised there are any Rugrats left, the way she carries on. Certainly their development seems to be a mite arrested, as Tommy has been in nappies for as long as I can remember. Even in fiction, parents don't get it right.

So if I could invent a set of perfect parents what would they be like? Obviously this is a totally theoretical exercise as they don't exist, and it's interesting that in the most popular children's fiction parents are conspicuous by their absence, so kids evidently think they can do pretty well without us. I have a vague sense that mothers ought to be wise and caring and bake bread and wear flowered aprons and regularly have a shampoo and set. But then the ideal mother should, as well as having the perfect shoulder to cry on, be able to make a farty noise with her underarm and lasso a bullock. A cross between Louisa May Alcott and Calamity Jane. Likewise fathers must be a mixture of the Director General of the United Nations and the Fonz: clever but cool. Parents in general should be intelligent, fun-loving, always considerate and never embarrassing. They should be experienced in life and ready with an answer to any difficult question; they must be patient and practical and have excellent ball skills. They should be able to conduct field operations, build a Wendy house, perform live theatre and know how to survive in the wild. They should also have access to a massive unearned income while taking care not to be over-indulgent.

Even if we did manage all that, our children would still probably find reasons to abuse us, so it's probably OK to limit ourselves to whatever we can cope with. I'm quite good with puppets but my surgical skills are limited to a dab of Savlon. I don't think Tolstoy was entirely right when he said 'All happy families are alike, but an unhappy family is unhappy after its own fashion'. I know what he meant, but isn't it also true that all families get along after their own fashion and no two are entirely alike? I know I can and do get unfairly judgmental about other people's styles of child-rearing, but (with the exception of martyrs, with whom I will have no truck) it doesn't seem to matter whether, as a parent, you are strict, jolly, disorganised or downright deluded – the job gets done. That boy who was allowed to play football in an art gallery, for example, hasn't turned into a moron, but an oxymoron: he is now a pleasant teenager. So perhaps I ought to stop sneering at other struggling parents and admit that it'll all come out in the wash. That is, of course, if you use *my* foolproof method of first soaking stains in cold water and laundry bleach (available in John Lewis) before a normal cycle in the machine...

Chapter Thirteen

War and peas

HOWEVER YOU CHOOSE TO GO ABOUT BRINGING up baby there is one tedious and repetitive task that no parent can ignore. They've got to be fed. Regularly. Otherwise there's no end of trouble. And since our daughter was born it's been the most regular area of conflict in our relationship. Why, if eating is supposed to be such a pleasure, isn't it?

It started well enough. I was a bit apprehensive about breast-feeding, having heard so many stories about women having unspecified 'trouble' in doing it and having to be shown by various professionals how to make your baby do what I assumed came naturally. Nipple, mouth, mouth, nipple. Once the introductions were made that was it, wasn't it? Luckily, my daughter was of the same opinion and compensated for my appalling ignorance by latching on like a limpet within minutes of birth. It was just as well one of us knew what she was doing. In the early days I was pleased to discover that she liked her grub and she liked her kip – definitely her mother's daughter. In fact she was so good at feeding she could do it for hours on end, which is why I soon decided that among all the essential baby equipment new parents are forced to buy, one of the items you really can't do without is a cordless phone. As soon as she started up the wailing I soon got the hang of arranging not only myself and the baby but a range of items (phone, book, remote control, drink, nourishing snacks) that I might feel the need for during the next hour or two. Another mistake I made was assuming that I would need plenty of clothes that unbuttoned at the front so that madam's requirements could be accommodated with speed and efficiency. Wrong again. Having become accustomed to whip out a nipple at a moment's notice I realised that just hiking up a large T-shirt is by far the quickest and most discreet way to get the job done. I've breast-fed in public countless times without ever once frightening the horses or getting invited on to *Kilroy* because nobody knew what I was doing. She was pink and white and fed all over. She's even been breast-fed underwater, if you count the Channel tunnel, and was very nearly sat on by a German tourist once, who didn't realise that there was a far more important drinking session going on right next to him.

And I liked it. Admittedly she made it easy for me by

doing what she was supposed to without the health visitor having to spell it out for her, but I remember looking at my healthy, glowing three-month-old girl and thinking, 'That's from me. I have nourished her with my own body' and smirking with pride. I even insisted on expressing some milk so that her father could experience the joy of feeding his own flesh and blood and seeing her happy, grateful little face staring up at him.

Nine months later I had an overpowering urge to slap her off my chest as if she was a noxious parasite and yell 'For God's sake get off me!' If getting her on to the breast was a dream, getting her off it was a bloody nightmare. I had hideous visions of her running up to me at four years old demanding 'Booby, booby!' I had heard of such hopeless cases and the thought that it might happen to me made me wake up in a cold sweat. Getting her to sleep during the day used to be easy, but without her comfort suck she yelled and screamed and pummelled me with her little fists as if I had suggested putting her to work in a coal mine instead of a refreshing nap, while I gamely sang 'Hush little baby...' and tried to ignore my aching breasts – bruised on the outside and swelling from the inside. If she could have spoken she would probably have pointed out in high dudgeon, 'Look, I can see it seeping through the front of your T-shirt. You're wasting that when I could be having it!'

My own body was conspiring against me, producing

masses of milk that I didn't want her to have. When my brain was sobbing 'Enough!' my breasts were wheedling, 'Oh, just a little bit more can't harm her. In some desert tribes breast-feeding carries on until five or six years old.' My brain growled back, 'It's not as if it's her only source of food, so she's not bloody well having it', and my ears tried to retreat inside my head to avoid the deafening screams of my deprived daughter.

My brain was right, for once. We had long since embarked on the fascinating journey that is weaning, which is when I made the interesting discovery that banana makes indelible stains. I never knew that. But then, I do tend to just eat bananas, not mash them up and smear them all over myself. During that happy time I adapted the Quentin Crisp approach to housework to my clothes. No point in washing anything until she has fish. Then I'll just walk through the car wash.

Weaning. The start of a long downward spiral, if you ask me. Getting constantly covered in gloop and goo should have given me some intimation that this feeding lark, once started, is hardly ever going to be unalloyed pleasure. The occasional spasm of relief, maybe, when fruit wins over fizzy pops, but mostly it's just what everyone says it shouldn't be: a battle.

God knows I tried. All the books will tell you that if you wean your child on lots of different foods it will be much more likely to eat a nutritious and varied diet when it gets the chance to express a preference. Most mothers will tell you it doesn't make a blind bit of difference. I liquidised the entire contents of Sainsbury's fruit and vegetable section (not all at the same time, obviously) and got it down her throat one way or another (not all of it, obviously). I dutifully peeled and cooked and mashed and puréed and nary a jar or packet was opened in our house. I cleaned the walls and floor and her clothes and my clothes and looked forward to the day when I would see her voluntarily tucking into asparagus and artichokes without chucking it all round the room. I was doing all the right things again and I congratulated myself.

Until the day when the ceiling fell down. With a kitchen that looked like a war zone and likely to remain so for some time while the insurance company cranked itself into action, I had to compromise on the feeding front and bought some jars of ready-made baby food. Not up to my standard of cooking, of course, but she wouldn't have to put up with it for long. With the first spoonful, which I assumed she would reject as 'Shop-bought. Not the same as home made', her face said 'Oh, *this* is nice. Why don't I get this all the time? Does it take the ceiling to fall down for me to get some decent food around here?' The sweet potatoes shrivelled in the vegetable basket and my hopes of a gourmet daughter shrivelled with them.

Despite the fact that it was situated far nearer to my waist than previously, at least I could call my chest my own again, but having struggled to wean her off it, even I occasionally hankered after the days when it was all so simple. In the words of an unknown schoolgirl, 'The advantages of breast milk are that it is convenient, cheap and the cat can't get at it.' To which I might add, it is almost always exactly the right temperature and you very rarely have to clean it off the walls. Fiddling about with plastic spoons and bibs and trying to get yoghurt out of her hair was always a bit of a chore. Besides which, when trying to shovel in liquidised organic carrot I sometimes looked at it and thought, 'Frankly, if this is her first taste of proper food I'm not surprised she's not wildly enthusiastic about it.' Babies' introduction to the exciting world of tastes and textures is pap. I wish I could have explained to her that she just had to get through this boring bit and then she could have spare ribs, Lobster Thermidor and – best of all – chocolate.

Her first chocolate biscuit was presented with great ceremony during her first Christmas on earth. The event was so momentous that we took photos. Actually, it wasn't the event itself but the sight of her chocolate-smeared face that was worth recording. Chocolate is, I think it is generally agreed, one of the finest pleasures in life. Of course our girl was going to enjoy it, too, but we solemnly and stupidly agreed that she was only going to get the finest Swiss or

Belgian confections so that she would learn to appreciate the taste of real chocolate and not just guzzle down any old Dairy Milk. What a couple of idiots. Five years on and I wonder what happened to that particular resolution (among many) and then I remember. Other people happened.

A (childless) friend told me that she knew somebody who never gave her children sweets and they grew up favouring cashew nuts over Curly Wurlys and if offered a box of Milk Tray would plump for a nice juicy apple instead. I think my response was 'Mm', while I was thinking 'Oh yeah? Where does this friend of yours live? Midwich?' I didn't believe a word of it, and even if it was true, then that mother must have managed it only by having 'Nil by mouth' tattooed on her children's foreheads. I have no objection to my daughter having treats, but there is a difference between a bar of Lindt and something that consists almost entirely of chemicals and food colouring. Among the things that were introduced into her diet by other people are crisps, sweet lollies and some sort of chewy squares that she claims are 'delicious'. And it's not just well-meaning but interfering friends and relatives who undermine all my best efforts. I'm under siege from the food industry and I'm threatening to put a ban on commercial television after the Fruit Winders incident. She saw an advert for the damn things and started clamouring to have them on the grounds that 'they've got fruit in them'. Unthinkingly I put some in the shopping basket and she'd eaten them before I discovered what they really were. My fault, of course, but I didn't realise the enormity of my mistake until I refused to buy any more of such rubbish. By that time she'd got the taste for them, and it was like trying to persuade a man-eating tiger that apples are an equally delicious food source. Real fruit doesn't seem to have the same addictive qualities, and I've never heard her begging and pleading for strawberries as much as she will for some strawberry-flavoured junk.

And as she got older I was more often required to hand over to other people the responsibility of getting her fed – some of whom were more responsible than others. Two of our more spectacular failures as au pairs were both really clueless about food. One was constantly moaning about her weight and would eat nothing but apple turnovers, Diet Coke and biscuits. She told me I shouldn't fry anything because it was really bad for me. She never did understand the difference between olive oil and lard, but made herself sick drinking cider vinegar because she thought it would make her thin. I told her she wasn't fat, but, bored with trying to explain basic truths to her, omitted to add that hip bones don't reduce in size whatever you do, and it's not a good idea to encase them in satin trousers that are two sizes too small. I didn't want my daughter's evening meal to be provided by someone who thought that a Terry's chocolate orange constituted a portion of fruit, so she had to go.

The next one never complained about being too fat, and swanned about in tiny little clothes and rollerblades. It was only when we discovered that whatever she ate (including chocolate spread by the shovelful in the middle of the night) she immediately sicked up again, that we decided she too had to go. Neither of them had any idea about how to feed themselves, let alone a child, and both of them were appalling examples to a small girl. That's all I needed: not only 'I don't like it' but 'I won't eat it because it might make me fat'. A truly frightening prospect.

As if it isn't hard enough trying to feed a child a balanced diet I'm fighting a losing battle against countless external influences. Why, for example, is it necessary to eat anything at all when watching a film in the cinema, let alone a bag full of E-numbers that cost more than the bloody ticket? Why will she turn her nose up at a perfectly decent bit of Cheddar yet demand to have some processed muck in her lunchbox because it's got a funny picture on the packet? Why do crisps and snacks take up an entire aisle in the supermarket? Why are burgers so inexplicably popular? Actually, I have to say that this is one tyranny that I seem to have escaped. She won't go near the clown's offerings, and I like to think that it's because she dimly remembers when all she ever got to eat was pap and is not about to go down that road again. This is despite the fact that a neighbour once took her for a burger, remarking spitefully, 'You don't think that you're going to be the only one to escape, do you?' I let her go, counting on the fact that she wouldn't touch a mouthful of a pappy meal, sorry, happy meal, and I was right. Apart from the odd bag of chips, pizzas are my only major concession to fast food, and although I got quite snotty about her referring to Pizza Hut as a restaurant, I had to admit that at least you get to eat with metal cutlery.

But I can't claim any moral high ground here. It's just my sheer good luck that she doesn't like burgers or Coke, she eats plenty of other rubbish, when she eats anything at all. The list of foods that she doesn't like grows steadily longer by the day, as she regards with deep suspicion anything vaguely new and will suddenly reject something that had previously been a favourite – usually just after I have bought in extra stocks of it. The conversations are wearyingly predictable:

'I don't like it.'

'How do you know if you've never tried it?'

'It doesn't look as if I'd like it.'

'Just try a bit.'

'Yuk, disgusting.'

The urge to give her nothing at all for a few days until she starts begging for cabbage and lentils is sometimes very strong, but I usually try to find something she likes, just to get anything in her stomach. Before I had a daughter I once heard a woman on the *Today* programme whose son would only ever eat jam sandwiches – absolutely nothing else. 'Stupid woman,' I thought. 'She's just not trying hard enough to make him eat properly.' How cruelly, if you'll excuse the pun, I have been made to eat my words. In vain her father will assure me that he ate nothing when he was a kid; in vain I hear the same story from other mothers – I'm convinced there must be something I can do to make her like spinach. Or anything, in fact. When she was much smaller she must have been the only child in the country who refused to eat ice-cream. I don't know why – it looked too brown, probably, so I actually found myself trying to encourage her to suck on a cornet when she didn't want to. 'I can't believe you're doing this,' her father said to me, and I didn't know why I was doing it, except it seemed unnatural for a two-year-old not to want to dive head first into chocolate ice-cream. As she has since got through the equivalent of about two swimming pools full of Mr Whippy I don't know why I did bother, except to use it as a weapon against her the next time she refuses to eat something because she doesn't think she's going to like it. 'Ha! You used to say that about ice-cream!' No doubt she simply wouldn't believe me.

A child that won't eat ice-cream could be classed as slightly odd. All her other reactions to food, however, could have come out of the toddler textbook. It's part of a mother's makeup to want her child to have three square meals a day – you're not doing your job properly unless you turn a little bit Jewish about it. Her idea of a balanced diet, however, was to tear about all day long like a mad thing fuelled only by half a piece of toast and two cornflakes. Occasionally she would surprise me by clearing her plate, but usually, most of what I dutifully served up would go in the bin – whatever wasn't surreptitiously introduced into my own diet. Now, it wouldn't occur to me to suggest that Captain Birdseye supply our evening meal, but half a fish finger left on the side of a plate always presented an over-whelming temptation to me to just pop it into my mouth – a temptation I rarely resisted. They're quite nice, actually, so I can't understand why there were ever any left on the side of the plate.

It could be that she refused to eat the rest of the fish finger because it had accidentally touched a pea. While not displaying typical toddler behaviour she would also some-times remind me of a caricature of a British tourist: won't touch anything 'mucked about with'. Any hint of herbs or condiments were regarded much as if I had sprinkled dead flies over her food, and had to be scraped and picked off before she would even look at it. Beans on toast were acceptable, but only if served on separate plates, so it was more like beans *beside* toast. Basically, anything out of a packet was probably OK, anything out of a saucepan, let alone a casserole, was sniffed at. Literally, before being pronounced 'disgusting'.

And if she did develop a sudden yen for something I approved of, it was usually when it was out of season. If I balked at the price of the strawberries she had spotted in Safeways in mid-December she would express slight disappointment. So I, of course, would shell out the frightening price for tasteless fruit, just because she wasn't asking for Jammie Dodgers. And then I'd still feel guilty because I was perpetuating the idea that everything is always available all year round and not explaining to her the importance and tastiness of seasonal food. Such a shame that crisps don't have a shorter growing season.

This refusal to eat anything vaguely unfamiliar was not only deeply troubling for a neurotic mother, it also necessitated extra planning at every turn. If I go out for the day and I get hungry, I either stay hungry or I buy something to eat. With a picky child on my hands, I had to be sure I always had a supply of tasty and nourishing snacks readily available, in case she suddenly got peckish and the only acceptable fodder on sale was biscuits or sweets. Every trip to the shops that took more than fifteen minutes, every afternoon in the park, meant that I had to pack a lunchbox full of carrot sticks and wholemeal sandwiches so I could quell any hunger pangs without having to resort to the sweet shop, because the greengrocer is obviously a no-go area when you've got the munchies and unless Mum has something to stuff in your mouth immediately the chocolate arguments are going to start. After all, no child in its right mind will enter a shop packed to the ceiling with crisps and sweets in full view and opt for a packet of raisins. Eating out was hopeless. We were once invited to an afternoon party at my boss's house and I foresaw trouble. Hell, she's not going to give quiche or salad a second glance. She oversaw the packing of her lunchbox on that occasion, and I had to undergo the humiliation of seeing my daughter serenely chewing on dry cornflakes and her own sandwiches while sitting at a table that was creaking under the weight of delicious home-made party food, none of which she would touch. Our hostess had gone to no end of trouble to feed us, but did it bother our girl? Not one whit. Dry cornflakes was what she wanted and dry cornflakes was what she had. Perhaps nobody would have noticed amid the party crowd, except that I, of course, felt it necessary to offer cringing apologies and so drew attention to my nutritionally challenged daughter.

I'm always envious of people whose children are good eaters. Not to say I believe celebrity chefs whose kids just can't get enough of goat's milk cheese and chicory, but surely a child who stank of garlic at six months old should be a little more cosmopolitan about her diet. Now it's the cat who stinks of garlic because he's quite willing to wolf down the leftovers – sometimes before they've actually been left over, if we're foolish enough to leave the table unattended for a nanosecond. It's not as if she's not interested in food – she'll always be eager to lend a hand with the cooking – it's just that she won't eat what she's cooked. Which is ridiculous, because we ate it after she'd sneezed in it, so I don't know what her problem is. She really does enjoy cooking very much. Very, very much. We were a little taken aback and didn't know whether to call Nigella Lawson or a child psychiatrist when we both witnessed her, up to her elbows in meatloaf mix, squeezing raw mince and egg through her fingers and whispering fiercely 'Yes! Yes!' It was one of those moments when you decide to just ignore it and say nothing. Trying to analyse, or even explain, her behaviour on that occasion would have been just too spookily worrying.

I really was forced to eat disgusting food when I was a girl (cheese pie, semolina, heart) which is why it's so annoying when she's fussy about food. So far, though, nothing she has done is particularly out of the ordinary. Nothing that would merit an appearance on the *Today* programme, anyway. When she was a toddler I had to keep repeating to myself that no child is voluntarily going to starve itself into malnutrition, and just tried to make sure that food was available immediately when she decided that she thought she could fancy a little something. I suppose children through the ages have poked at their plates, refused to eat their greens and fed stuff to the dog, it's just that they didn't have oven chips and Fruit Winders to fill in the gaps. If my daughter doesn't eat as well as I would like it's probably my own fault for not spending hours slaving over hot allotments and steaming pastry boards. Those clever marketing people know perfectly well that few of us have time to be Delia or Jamie – hence microwave meals and cartoon yoghurts, which of course, children will choose every time over something with a picture of fruit on the label. (At least she knows the colour of spaghetti. I was about twelve before I saw any that wasn't orange and out of a tin. It came as a great surprise.) So I serve up smiley faces and chicken nuggets and hope that some time in the distant future my daughter will be savouring gorgonzola and gentleman's relish. I remember the fuss we all used to make when our father got the smelly cheese out: all rushing from the room holding our noses and making exaggerated vomit noises. What I *don't* remember is the first time I ever actually ate any, but as I can now shovel pounds of the stuff down my gullet I assume there must be hope for my daughter's palate.

So I'm not going to give up. Every so often she surprises, not to say astonishes, me by pouncing ravenously on sunflower seeds or watermelon and I can say joyously

'Yes! Have as much as you like!' Most of the time it's a war of attrition against the attractions of crisps and Cadbury's Chocolate Fingers. I do my bit. Every time she gets a packet of Pringles I try to eat as many of them as possible. It's not that I want them, you understand, it's just that the more I eat, the less there are for her. It's a sacrifice I'm willing to make in order to save her from herself. That's how caring a mother I am: I will finish off a tube of Smarties in one gulp while slicing raw carrot for her. How much more dedicated to her welfare could I be?

Chapter Fourteen

Mrs Entertainment

SO WHAT IF THE DINING TABLE HAS BECOME a battleground? In between mealtimes are playtimes. Nothing but fun, fun, fun! Time to stimulate the baby's synapses with a challenging session of peek-a-boo – she'll be playing chess in no time. Do all young animals play? Do mother lions and horses say to their scampering offspring 'Not now, darling, I've got to chase an antelope/eat a bale of hay?' Have other human mothers stared into the windows of Hamleys and wondered 'What's the point of a stuffed hippo?'?

A playing kitten is learning to rend and tear bird flesh (and sometimes human flesh) as it performs its amusing antics. A playing child is similarly learning just about every-thing useful to its future life. A playing mother can sometimes forget that, start looking at her watch, get bored and distracted and suggest a nice game of going to sleep for a couple of hours.

I thought I was quite good at playing when my daughter was little. I found it surprisingly – not to say worryingly – easy to act like an idiot and roll around the floor shrieking. I found ways to entertain her all day long, and even if Teletubbies played their part in keeping her amused, I was there for her the rest of the time, making sure she wasn't getting bored. There were times when I needed a trip to the park like a hole in the head, but there was always something to absorb the attention of a toddler. I have to admit, though, that nursery school came just in time to save me from reaching the limits of my imagination or patience. I could do finger painting or junk modelling or sticklebricks as well as anybody else, but I was just about ready to hand the job over to the professionals. There was no way I could supply her with a playground full of equipment, let alone a couple of dozen playmates to muck about with, so I was very happy for her to toddle off and make an appalling mess under somebody else's roof, so I could abandon play with relief and get back to the much more interesting pastime of working.

I've had some fabulous times playing with my daughter. Sometimes it makes you remember that there is a point to a stuffed hippo if it can be thrown around, made to do amusing things with funny voices and make a small child laugh like a drain. That's why children like playing – it's fun. Pure fun, that doesn't involve alcohol (necessarily), intellect (necessarily) or proving a point (necessarily). So why, when we could spend all day just fooling around, did I ever feel the need to do the washing up or hoover the carpet? Because I thought I had to do that as well, I suppose, so her playtimes were too often curtailed by the siren call of Mr Sheen, when it really shouldn't have mattered. It's strange, isn't it, that I had the perfect opportunity to spend all my days doing nothing but playing, but I didn't actually want to. Having spent years complaining about the tedium of working, now I was grouching about having to spend so much time playing. What a complex mass of contradictions I must be. But the laundry still had to be done.

Before I started trying to combine childcare and house-work I could never understand for the life of me why anybody would buy a child a toy ironing board. What on earth is the point of pretending that ironing is fun? I looked further and found that almost everything can be reduced to the status of a toy: hoovers, lawnmowers, tills, mobile phones (God help us), earth-moving equipment, sewing machines, law enforcement uniforms and first aid kits. Toy scrubbing brushes? What next? Toy welding kits? Toy nuclear reactors? I really thought the Early Learning Centre had lost it, until I twigged – Mary Poppins was right again.

Every household task contains an element of fun. Actually, this is a complete lie, there is nothing remotely entertaining about a pile of bone-dry wrinkled clothes, but if the ironing has to be done and the kid wants to play, obviously the answer is to persuade her that this is just another game and she can copy Mummy with her own little ironing board. I'm *really* not convinced about this so I always just left the ironing until she was asleep. I feel as if it's lying to children to pretend that doing the hoovering or cutting the grass is anything other than boring work and they should be out chasing butterflies and imagining themselves flying to the moon, not replicating in play activities that will be hateful to them in the future. Unless, of course, they are destined to become lepidopterists or astronauts, in which case they'll have plenty of time in adult life to hunt insects or rocket into space and doing a little light dusting might be seen as a pleasant break from routine.

When you haven't thought about them for a few decades, toys can be fascinating, especially if you believe the manufacturers' claims about improving hand-to-eye co-ordination: they are in fact less playthings and more educational tools (although I've yet to see one that's actually called 'How not to stick your finger in your eye'). This could lead you to believe that you were really going to turn your kid into a rocket scientist rather than just buying a rattle. A lot of toys, though, are irritating bits of hideously coloured plastic that squeak or whistle or need batteries and are held together with tiny screws that fall out and get eaten. And however exciting they might be when the wrappers come off, they don't usually hold the attention for that long. We do have one notable exception to the rule, however. When our daughter was a year old a friend gave her a toy that has really stood the test of time. It's just four coloured balls that you hit with a mallet so they fall through holes and down a slope. Then you collect them all from where they've rolled into corners and under chairs and do it again. Naturally, it's supposed to improve hand-to-eye co-ordination but basically it's just bashing. She loved that toy, and strangely, so did everyone else. 'Ooh, can I have a go?' they would say as soon as they clapped eyes on it; then they would spend a few minutes indulging in deeply satisfying walloping. I wasn't immune myself, but couldn't figure out why it was so pleasurable. A highly trained psychiatrist might attempt an explanation, once you could wrest the little plastic mallet out of his or her hand. We've still got it, and every time I threaten to consign it to the charity shop with the words 'It's a *baby* toy!' she wails 'But Mummy I like it!' I remember all those thoroughly engrossed adults and think she might have a point, so back it goes into the toy cupboard.

Another abiding favourite among all the discarded bits of plastic and ugly dolls is Polly the cat. As no great fan of soft toys, even I have a soft spot for Polly, who has been part of our lives since our daughter was only a few days old. She's getting a bit woolly round the armpits now, but she will never see the inside of an Oxfam shop or bin bag as long as there is breath in our bodies. The only problem with Polly is her colour. This is probably not the place to drag up all those bitter arguments that cause such lifelong rifts between cat-lovers, but I'm sure it was the close association with Polly for all those years that caused our daughter, when given the choice of a litter of perfectly beautiful oriental kittens, to choose the ginger one. As we walked away her father remarked bitterly, 'A hundred and twenty quid and we've got a fucking ginger cat.' Never underestimate the power of a soft toy over a child's psyche. (Actually, he's not really ginger – he's an *oriental red*. That's posh ginger – and the rest of the Spice Girls rolled into one. He probably weighs more.)

But apart from bashing and stroking, games of all sorts – involving toys or not – are part of her playtime, whether it be snakes and ladders, shop assistants, pretending to be dogs or re-tiling the bathroom. Whether I get roped into it or not is not entirely of my own choosing. I enjoy a game as much as the next man, but sometimes it's not a question of having other things to do, it's just that crawling around the floor barking doesn't hold much appeal. It doesn't seem to matter, either, that I'm clearly not really throwing myself into my role as shop assistant (unless it's bored shop assistant) or doctor, and I couldn't care less what she buys or how many broken legs she's got. As long as I'm there, impatiently going through the motions, it is obviously fulfilling one of the most important functions of play: preparing her for a lifetime full of bored shop assistants and impatient doctors – not to mention rather snappy dogs and incompetent plumbers. And if I can sometimes see the appeal of a stuffed hippo, I failed entirely to see the significance of a plastic pizza with the slices held together with Velcro. She knew, though. It exists so that I can pretend to be a waitress serving a rather demanding customer. (And I didn't even get a tip.)

When I've really had enough of course I do what I hope most mothers do and fall back on the television. Actually I fall back on the sofa and grope wildly for the remote control, hoping that something suitable will catch her attention and I can persuade her to stare at a screen for as long as it takes me to collect my energies. Some children's television is in fact quite good, and I can tell myself that there is no harm at all in her watching her favourite 'doing and making' pro- grammes (until she wants to do and make it all at home). Some of it is complete crap, but that doesn't stop me from letting her watch it, even if it does mean I later have to endure explanations of the 'plots' of *Scooby-Doo* or *Woody Woodpecker* – both of which I was surprised to find were still 'entertaining' another generation of kids. Cartoons are apparently timeless, as I understood when I turned on the television before 7p.m. for the first time in years and up popped Secret Squirrel. An awful lot of recycling goes on in children's television and I'm sure that Zoë Ball was thrilled to know that she was still appearing on our screens until quite recently in a knitted tank top with well-brushed hair, reading a story to a bunch of bored nose-pickers. Has there ever been anybody in the history of television who has decided to make an entire career as a kids' TV presenter, or is it always just a stepping stone to something else, such as presenting Crufts or taking cocaine? Only Toyah seems to be the exception to the rule. From punk queen to the voice of the Teletubbies – you can't say she's not versatile. Other offerings for kids, such as *Andy Pandy* and *Bill and Ben*, have undergone more subtle changes – like not being in black and white any more – and one in particular appeared in our sitting room less like an old friend and more like an unwelcome guest.

Blue Peter has been around very nearly as long as I have. I grew up under the calming influence of Valerie Singleton, John Noakes and Christopher Trace (or 'Sunk Without', as he came to be known). Imagine my surprise to find that while I went off and did other things, none of which involved sticky-backed plastic, *Blue Peter* stayed hidden and unwatched on my television set and it is still there. Only the faces have changed. The Advent candles certainly haven't. Given the time span presumably there are herds of ex-*BP* animals jostling for space in pet heaven, but really I couldn't tell the difference. You'll never see a borzoi or a bulldog on the *BP* set – it's always a bloody Labrador or a golden retriever and a couple of nondescript (possibly drugged) cats. The presenters pull the same stunts as ever, involving jumping off things, getting wet, getting earnest, asking possibly quite interesting people inane questions and imparting vaguely interesting facts with the flimsy pretence that it's all 'amazing!' I swear I saw one once ask Quentin Blake what his favourite colour is. That's only a very slight exaggeration. The difference from my day is that the girls wear far fewer clothes than Valerie Singleton ever did even when she was in the bath, probably, and they get amazed in the sort of estuary English that would have had Lord Reith spitting with rage – if he could have under-stood them. Did I like it when I was a child? Or did I have that same sinking feeling that I have now: 'Ooh, what's on next? Is it one of those amusing Gabor Csupo cartoons that are fun for all the family? Oh. No. It's *Blue Peter.*'

Unfortunately my daughter has inherited my prejudices and cannot be persuaded to stay glued to the screen for hours on end. The familiar *BP* music is her cue to switch off the television and drag me out, screaming but not kicking, for a nice game of football. Bearing in mind that the garden isn't really big enough for a game of Subbuteo, this puts me in a bit of a quandary. If I suggest that we go the park to play, that might mean that I'd have to run about a bit and would be very likely to get slightly puffed. On the other hand, if I just stand in goal and get booted at, it's not only me who is in physical danger but all my carefully tended plants. The grass is a write-off, needless to say, but I'd quite like to keep the flowerbeds more than three inches high. Sometimes we compromise with badminton racquets and foam balls, but we have to buy the balls by the gross because of all the ones that disappear over the fence while the neighbours are out. When the last one goes sailing into the wide blue yonder (or Joyce's garden, as we call it) it's time for me to suggest something a little more cerebral, and I don't mean watching *Inspector Morse*.

Explaining board games was hard going at first, but well worth it in the end. Games and puzzles held an interest for her, once she had got past the peek-a-boo stage, but I was impatient for her to get on to jigsaws with more than six pieces and understand the rules of Ludo. Games of chance and skill combined are excellent for teaching children mathematics and logical thinking. Besides which, I had long since got bored with retrieving balls from under plants or over fences, and the idea of something we could both enjoy while sitting down (maybe with a glass of something revivifying to hand) was very, very appealing.

Maybe rules are made to be broken, but once she had grasped the concept of things being done in a certain way to make the game work, she also soon grasped the concept of being able to change the rules at will.

'We can play snakes and ladders, but we don't
  have to go down the really long snake.'

'I can have another go because I didn't mean to do
  that.'

'No, I don't have to throw a six to start.'

'You can't knock me out but I can knock you out.'
  (In reference to a board game, not a boxing
  match, fortunately.)

And when she wasn't changing the rules to suit herself, she was just plain cheating. The point of games is that sometimes, somebody wins. If it wasn't her, it was a cue for sulking and flouncing. So while she was learning the finer points of gamesmanship I struggled with my conscience. Should I just allow her to win and avoid trouble, or try harder so that she would learn how to lose gracefully? I decided that her friends weren't going to indulge her criminal tendencies, so I'd better put the game on a proper footing and actually try to beat her. It took quite a few games, I have to say, before she accepted the fact that it was possible for Mummy to win occasionally, and the fun is supposed to be in the taking part, not in creaming the opposition. It's lucky that I'm not very competitive – there's something particularly unedifying about an adult with a will to win desperately trying to beat a five-year-old at tiddly-winks. So I let the roll of the dice decide which of us would triumph over the snakes and didn't race round the room with my shirt over my head when it was my turn to be victorious. Gracious in victory, resigned in defeat, that's me. Although the memory games tested my powers of benign resignation more than somewhat. Her numerous brain cells would invariably race ahead of my rapidly depleting collection and she regularly beat me hands down. 'You must concentrate, Mummy!' she giggled viciously as she swept the piles of cards over to her side of the table, and I grumbled about sheer luck and how winning wasn't really that important, but I would like to beat her *once* in a while. I don't think I ever have. After all my careful teaching about the fun being in the taking part, I looked a little foolish getting grouchy because I didn't stand a snowball's chance in hell of pasting the little madam in a stupid game I didn't want to play anyway.

Time to get out of the house before I started getting flouncy and sulky. A day out that's fun for all the family. Now that would be a first. A day out that incorporates splashing in water and splashing wine into large glasses; Italian ice-cream *and* Italian food; chocolate eclairs and Jenny Eclair; a ride on a carousel and the National Theatre production of it – that's a good day out for *all* the family. I've never been to Alton Towers, but despite the advertisements full of happy smiling families I don't think I have been denying myself a good time. A family day out is usually more fun for one member of the family in particular than it is for the rest of us, and yet we do it because the kids love it. Of course there is vicarious satisfaction in seeing my daughter having a great time, but I can't deny there is a certain amount of parental sacrifice involved as well. My idea of a good day on the beach includes a lot of lying around doing nothing, interspersed with quick dips and cold beers. It has nothing to do with standing waist-deep in water chucking a ball around – that's not the way to get your legs brown. Zoos can be interesting (when they're not deeply troubling) but I remember her father in a right old strop when he brought her back from a 'fun day out'. He had just spent a fortune taking her to London Zoo where she had spent most of her time in a playground that was exactly the same as the one in the local park. After another long day in a different zoo she declared her favourite animals to be the stray cats that strolled around the grounds and ate the penguins' food: 'Because I stroked one.' An entire day filled with exotic and amusing animals, chips, popcorn, ice-cream, a clown show, playgrounds, falling in the paddling pool and a ride on a chair lift and the highlight was some scabby old fleabag that was probably fizzing with bacteria. You can't say we don't know how to show her a good time.

But it doesn't always have to be a whole day of mind-numbing, knackering child entertainment. Sometimes half an hour of it can reduce me to the same painfully bored state, a sure sign of which is when I start tugging at her sleeve and whimpering 'Can we go now?'

I've seen some very good children's entertainers and I've seen some outrageously bad ones. It seems to depend on whether they have been employed by somebody very rich or by the council. We both once sat politely and watched the excruciating efforts of a clown in the local playcentre. It was free, but frankly he should have paid us for not throwing things. What he lacked in talent, skill and sense of humour he made up for with a large amount of false ginger hair. At least I think it was false. If it was real I suppose it would explain why he thought he was fitted to be a children's entertainer: no other career would be open to him.

Anyway, we watched stony-faced as he performed his hilarious antics and when release finally came we shuffled off with relief to go and watch some paint dry. Still slightly dazed by the sort of performance that was only a whisker away from child abuse (it was certainly parent abuse) I asked my daughter, 'Did you think he was funny?' With a critic's disdain worthy of Brian Sewell she replied 'Not really' and then cackled derisively. I almost felt sorry for the talentless sod. It can't do much for your self-esteem to be despised by a five-year-old.

Luckily it's not all that bad. We trained her from a very early age to appreciate the cinema. Unfortunately this meant missing large chunks of some quite good films because she was a bit *too* young to sit through the whole thing. *Toy Story 2* was the turning point, and by the time the second Harry Potter film came out she was a confirmed fan of the silver screen, willing to sit through to the bitter end. It was me who was fidgeting. Oh. A monster. I expect he's going to kill it. Are they going to make *Shrek 2*? There's been time while this film's been on.

And theatre. We do theatre, too, but in shifts. She's seen plenty of children's shows, but her first grown-up theatre was going to see *Bombay Dreams* with her father, which she loved, but kept on asking when I was going to take her again, because I hadn't seen it. 'Well, best-beloved, I didn't come with you because your father has just kissed goodbye to the best part of sixty quid just for a matinée (and a CD). Maybe when I get paid I'll think about it. When is Granny next visiting?' Instilling a love of live theatre is a wonderful idea. Getting somebody else to pay for it is an even better idea.

Toys, books, games, television, videos, days out, cinema and theatre trips, clowns and kittens and kites – above it all towers the pinnacle of children's entertainment: the party.

The once-a-year bash that my daughter starts planning about six months before the event and I cobble together in about six days. The first one, of course, was run like a military operation, before I realised that all they wanted to do was rush around screaming and get a party bag before they went home. There are certain elements that they have to have: a cake, games and a small amount of blood and tears. Otherwise I decided I could forget about magicians, bouncy castles and colour themes – a large outdoor space with things to play on and ice-cream on tap was all they needed to get hysterically over-excited and think they were having a good time. Why get sucked into the whirling vortex that is party organisation when the kids are not, frankly, terribly discriminating? It doesn't seem to matter whether it's at Burger King or Buckingham Palace – tell them it's a party and they throw themselves into the spirit of the thing with never a complaint about the state of the canapés or the fact that the napkins don't match. I maintain that unless your idea of a children's party is to sit them down and explain the theory of relativity, it's much easier than a lot of parents seem to think it is. In fact, a children's party is not much like a party at all. Apart from the cousins from out of town they all know each other and don't need to make small talk. There's no polite conversation, precious little networking and nothing at all that could remotely be called dancing. The food is crap and the music is worse (and it keeps on stopping). Obviously, there will always be at least one with an obsessive personality who doesn't know when to stop and lavish vomiting may happen, but apart from that, these occasions bear little resemblance to anything that I would call a marvellous party. And yet they love them. Our daughter had a great time at her last party, despite the fact that half the guests had forgotten to tell their mothers about the invitations and I was getting calls for weeks afterwards saying 'I'm terribly sorry we missed the party but Tom/Dick/Harriet has only just told me about it.' I secretly think that my daughter's had just as much fun with her parents and a CD player, arsing about in the sitting room, but because it was called Tuesday night, and not a party, it didn't count.

Play. What is it good for? Absolutely everything, really. A doll or a soft toy can teach them about nurturing and caring and the fact that only *stuffed* cats can go in the washing machine. Games with other children are excellent for learning social skills, whether it be the simple act of sharing toys, or Machiavellian plans for humiliating the other team (which is much more fun). Any outdoor activities, such as football, rollerblading or climbing trees, are important for making their little bodies grow straight and strong and all teach the valuable lesson that iodine stings like buggery. A little grit in the knee puts iron in the soul.

Board games – logical thinking, strategy, the power of luck, the terrible realisation that luck is also dependent on mathematics and we are not ever going to win the Lottery.

Cinema, theatre, the zoo, the adventure playground – it's all there to give them a good time and teach them valuable life skills. Even clowns can be useful in developing critical faculties. More importantly for any mother trying to keep a child entertained, however, is that all this activity is also guaranteed to get them so knackered that they'll go to bed early. Result. Well, half a result, because I usually end up wanting to go to bed about twenty minutes after she has, with rather painful ball-related injuries and a vague sensation of having given good fun but not actually having had any myself. (I must remember to compare notes with some prostitutes on this matter.) I dare say that when she's loaded down with homework and when she does have any free time wouldn't be seen dead with her clapped-out old mother I shall look back fondly to the times when I was her favourite playmate. Until then I'll slide down the snakes with good grace, buy in some more ground cover plants and improve my waitressing skills. What larks.

Chapter Fifteen

A Weak Solution

I T'S NOT ALL FUN AND GAMES, AS ANY FULE KNO, and as this fule knows only too well. We have not – yet – had to resort to child psychiatrists or the police, but we have our problems. And more often than not it's up to me to solve them.

Faced with a problem at work, say, I like to think that I'm quite good at not panicking or flying off the handle. I can follow logical thought processes, examine different plans of action and come up with some sort of solution. When I have a problem with my daughter I'm not so clear-headed. Could this be anything to do with the first realisation that my child wasn't perfect? It was a painful admission to make (one that some of us never actually get around to) and it easily led me into making mountains out of molehills, creating storms in teacups and generally worrying myself silly.

When our girl was small, problems, although they seemed life-threatening at the time, were not insurmountable. Mostly they involved sleep patterns, and what byzantine, spontaneous and complicated patterns they made. Think Jackson Pollock rather than Mondrian. Other little blips and glitches ruffled the smooth surface of our lives as well. The colic, the unwillingness to sleep when she was supposed to, the bizarre decision to get up and start her day at 4a.m., the hatred of mother and toddler group (hers, but to a certain extent mine as well), the sudden objection to the rain hood on the buggy, the lack of a healthy appetite, the deep suspicion of doting relatives – all these things have given me cause for concern at some point.

I couldn't do much about the rain hood except put it down when it was raining and push her, screaming and punching it, through the downpour. There was no solution to that problem, as I quickly realised when I caught myself trying to explain to a one-year-old fairly bellowing with rage that I simply didn't want her to get wet, as the rain dripped off my nose. Sorry dear, but if you don't like it, that's just tough, there's absolutely nothing I can do about it. Other problems, most notably sleep – or rather the lack of it – must surely have had some simple remedy, but I had to admit to being stumped. I had no idea how to stop a small child from waking up at some ungodly hour of the morning and wanting to play. We tried various techniques that didn't work until I was so desperately tired I couldn't stand it a minute longer. And she stopped doing it. It was a similar story when she suddenly took against having her nappy changed. Having previously been docile and manageable, she turned into an apparently eight-limbed beast and would struggle and squirm and roll all over the changing mat while I tried to restrain her kicking legs with one hand while with the other removing a smelly nappy without getting the contents on the walls and in my hair. I began to dread what had formerly been quite a simple operation until I had absolutely reached the end of my tether. And she stopped doing it.

I began to detect a pattern. She couldn't possibly know what she was doing and that I had just reached breaking point – could she? But she seemed to be able to read the mush that passed itself off as my mind at the time and change her behaviour just minutes before I gave her up for adoption. 'OK, I've had my fun and I've pushed her to the limit. I'd better stop now before I overstep the mark.' A more likely explanation was, of course, that the problems we had with her when she was a baby and tiny child were all a matter of time. Colic wears off; she won't always be wearing a nappy; she won't always be drinking from a trainer cup. If you strengthen your resolve, keep on doing what you have to and wait long enough these little problems will clear themselves up in time. And I never really reached the end of my tether, there was always a little bit more rope left. I may have developed a few hairline cracks but I never actually broke. So I just waited for time to do its work and it always did. I'll never forget the first time after her birth (a very long time after her birth) when I woke up one morning after a full eight hours of uninterrupted kip. I understood how Norwegians must feel when the spring arrives. I just never thought it would happen, but the world was still turning and there was light on the horizon. Eventually she would sleep through the night every night. 'This too will pass' was an often-repeated phrase, albeit through gritted teeth. If I just held myself steady and tried not to panic, things would sort themselves out. 'She'll grow out of it' was a handy crutch to lean on when things started getting sticky.

Unfortunately, it's not a philosophy that you can rely on forever. Hoping that some behavioural disorder will just go away is the parental equivalent of not opening your bank statements and can lead to equally dire consequences. As she got older I had to rely rather less on Old Father Time and more on Old Mother. I was forced to apply myself a little more, and as the usual logical thought processes don't work with children I adopted the well-used parental methods. A combination of threats, bribery and constant nagging.

Actually I'm pretty weak on threats. I can't issue threats in the nature of 'I will take your bike to the dump if you don't stop that' because I know I won't be able to carry them through. My threats are more likely to involve the consequences of her actions. 'If you don't have a bath you will smell.' If this worked and I did get her into the bath I might have to add: 'If you don't stop splashing water around it will seep through the floorboards, everything will rot and the house will fall down.' A little extreme, you might think, but it could happen, and she stopped splashing, and the house is still standing. Unfortunately, although she swallowed this one at bathtime, her faultless logic soon came into play. She wouldn't splash water in the bathroom at the top of the house, but it doesn't count in the kitchen on the ground floor, because houses fall down, not up. Wooden floors still rot, however, so when she'd been at the sink and I paddled into the kitchen there was no time for subtlety. I am most disapproving of the 'Wait till your father gets home' form of threat, but I think I was justified in shrieking 'Oh my *God!* We'd better get this cleaned up right away! If your dad sees this he'll go *spare!*'

The prospect of her father having kittens acts more as an interesting concept than a genuine threat, but sometimes the fear of ridicule is enough to stop her in her tracks as she careers off down the path of delinquency. Whatever ruses I might employ, whatever exhortations, threats or bribes I might try, sometimes the solution to a problem lies quite outside my sphere of influence. Fairly often, in fact, if I'm brutally honest. When I was trying to persuade her to ditch the buggy I could argue until I was blue in the face but she wouldn't listen to me, a mere parent.

'No you must walk to nursery, it's not very far.'

'But my legs get tired.'

'It's good for them.'

'I *need* to go in the buggy .'

'Nonsense, a big girl like you?'

And so on and so on. She still wanted to be carried around on wheels, and if there had been two people available to do the job she probably would have opted for a sumptuous litter with velvet curtains – anything so she wouldn't have to stir her stumps. Cajoling her into a nice, brisk walk just wasn't working. I knew all about unhealthy children who needed a lift to get to the ice-cream van and I could see her losing the use of her legs when she hadn't long found it. This was the start of a lifetime of laziness! If I couldn't convince her now, she would probably take to her bed in her mid-twenties and have to be lifted out of her room by crane! I was getting extravagant visions of a child on wheels and generally whipping myself up into a lather of anxiety. Eventually the only thing that convinced her to give it up was when I pointed out that *nobody else* came to nursery in a buggy – only baby brothers and sisters. It was the fear of pointing fingers that made her agree that she couldn't possibly be the only one in her class still being pushed around like a *baby*, and the buggy was finally abandoned. Mum had sod all to do with it. Likewise she hung on to a training beaker for far too long, just because she liked the picture on it, when she was well able to drink from a proper cup. Any suggestion of mine about a combination of beaker and bin would be met with loud and heartfelt protests, and I was getting myself all worked up with desperate imaginings of a sixteen-year-old whose drinking problem was that she would only do it through a spout. It was only when a friend of mine visited and remarked casually, 'Goodness, you're a bit old to be drinking from that cup, aren't you?' and I saw the look on my daughter's face, that I knew I could safely sling it. She'd been rumbled by an external source, and whatever I might have said, it took somebody else's chance remark to separate her from her beloved cup.

Another throwaway comment opened up a further avenue of threatening behaviour for me. Once, when she was being particularly troublesome and badly behaved, I said, 'Why are you doing this to me? You don't behave like this at school do you? What would your teacher think if I told him what you are like at home?' It was just a rhetorical question, and I had no intention of telling him what a complete cow his star pupil was in reality, but her obvious panic as she begged me '*Please* don't tell him' gave me another weapon to use against her. I can't use it very often, though, as eventually she will call my bluff, and I'm sure her teacher is supremely uninterested in whether or not she has written her thank-you letters, and wouldn't thank me for wasting his time in telling him about it.

Bribery is another well-worn method of improving behavioural standards, and one I have resorted to myself on occasions. The odd 'You can have an ice-cream if you promise not to make a fuss about having to go to the super-market' is a quick-fix solution designed to make things easier for me, but again, it can't be used too often otherwise she wouldn't do anything she was asked to without exacting a fee. As I once heard somebody say very sensibly when discussing bribery for children: 'The reward for tidying your room is having a tidy room.' I'm not averse to using bribery when it suits me but when a more serious situation arose it required more elaborate plans on my part. Not so long ago bedtimes were becoming more and more problematical, not to mention later and later. The combination of school holidays, light evenings and high energy levels meant that our daughter's bedtime 'routine' was shot to hell and unless we stayed up until 2a.m. there was precious little left of the evening for us to spend peacefully alone. Naturally I adopted my primary method of problem-solving and thought, 'Well, when she goes back to school she'll be more tired and it'll sort itself out.' Which made it ten times worse, of course, because now she had to get up in the morning as well, and I was getting more and more worried every evening as the clock ticked and she was still finding excuses not to brush her teeth.

Tethers were getting taut and pretty passes had been come to when somebody suggested the sticker system. Knowing her predilection for stickers I thought it might just work. So we made a chart and bought some stickers and I laid down the rules. In order to get a sticker she must be tucked up in bed at a reasonable hour having had a proper meal, done her homework (which only takes about five minutes), had a bath and brushed her teeth. Up until that point I was having great difficulty in accomplishing all these tasks before midnight, so one or more of them invariably went by the board if she was to get a proper night's sleep. After successfully earning fifteen stickers (which I calculated would take about a month) she was to get an unspecified 'prize'. My suggestion that this should be a big kiss didn't go down too well, and nor did her suggestion of a new bike. Still, there were a lot of stickers to get through and we could cross that bridge when we came to it.

On the first sticker evening she came home from school and was spectacularly sick all over the kitchen floor, the cupboards and my trousers. 'Right, well, I think we'll forget about the proper dinner tonight, but the rest still stands.' Slightly subdued by her extravagant but one-off barf, which thankfully didn't presage any major illness, she went to bed like a lamb and earned her sticker. Things went as planned for a couple of days, her chart was filling nicely and all tasks were completed. Then she started getting cocky. Bouncing into bed far later than she was supposed to, because she had been playing up, she demanded her sticker, which she now regarded as her right.

'No, you can't have a sticker tonight because you
    wouldn't go upstairs when I told you to.'

The wails and arguments and tears that followed somewhat defeated the object of the exercise. She obviously hadn't grasped the concept of bribery and just regarded her chart as a countdown to a large and expensive present.

'No, no, no, you don't get a prize for being bad,
    you get one for being *good*.'

I was aiming to put to bed a well-fed, clean and happy child. Instead of which I had a miserable little crosspatch on my hands who was going to be even more tired and peevish in the morning. This was supposed to be a positive reward system, not baksheesh, but she refused point-blank to understand my arguments and it took a few more fraught evenings to get back on track. What probably helped was not my efforts at all, but the discovery that her friend was being subjected to the same method and it became a competition as to who was winning the sticker race and who was going to get a bigger prize. I would at this point advise anybody considering this system to check with other mothers first whether or not they are doing the same thing and get your stories straight. A big bar of chocolate is going to look like a pretty piss-poor reward if somebody else in the class has been promised a live pony.

It did work to a certain extent, and we got to the end of the chart, which was when I discovered that all these early nights had given her boundless energy for shopping. We had compromised on a new top, but when I watched her carefully selecting armfuls of unsuitable clothes from the rails like a miniature Victoria Beckham I thought I might have replaced one problem with another. Now how was I going to stop her from turning into an acquisitive little fashion victim? About twenty-five quid and *more* than one new top later it also crossed my mind that there must be cheaper ways of regulating her behaviour.

Wearing her down with constant nagging sometimes does the trick, but I do find it a little wearisome as well. Saying the same thing over and over again is not my idea of fun, either, but surely she must get the message when she hears me say *again*: 'You *know* why you've got to clean your teeth – I've told you about a million times!' (This is classed as a combination of the nagging and threat of consequences methods.) What we hardly ever do when faced

with a problem is to sit down and discuss it. This is prima-
rily because usually what I perceive to be a problem she
regards as a great way to live her life. If she falls into bed at
nine o'clock with dirty feet that's a result as far as she's concerned – what's there to talk about? It's no good pointing out
the next day that if she feels tired it's her own fault for not
doing as she was told the night before – she simply won't
make the connection.

So we battle on with threats, bribes, nagging – and one
eminently practical solution that I hit upon quite by chance
and that has made bedtimes much less fraught and much
earlier. Now, if I feed the cat a large and heavy meal just
before her bedtime, he will invariably stagger off to her
bed to sleep it off. I can then point out that if the cat's tired
then so should she be, and she will dutifully bound off after
him and snuggle down to a lullaby of rich, throaty purring.
It's gratifying when I can occasionally find a solution that
works, is practical, cheap and doesn't involve too much
effort on my part. It's not so gratifying to have to admit that
she will totally ignore her mother but follow the cat's
example with alacrity (if I could just get him to do his
homework on time as well...). Some people might think
that the cat sleeping on her bed is a problem, but some
people can think what they bloody well like. It works.

If we don't sit down as a family and thrash out our
problems, I am also wary of discussing them in open forum.

'A problem shared is a problem halved' could also be interpreted as 'A problem shared gives somebody else the excuse to gloat over your misfortunes'. If I do share my problems with friends I don't do it to get help or advice. I just want a sympathetic ear and somebody to say 'Oh, you poor thing. They're little buggers, aren't they?' It gives me the strength to re-enter the fray to know that I'm not the only one experiencing a few setbacks, and it relieves my feelings a little to be able to wail 'I just don't know what to *do*!' without anyone feeling obliged to actually tell me. So when a third party is a disapproving witness to our daughter's errant behaviour I am always quick to point out, 'Yes, I am *aware* that this is not acceptable. I'm not ignoring it, I'm working on it, OK?' Naturally, these are the only times when she singularly fails to take account of independent opinion, and will make me cringe with embarrassment as she displays in public the sort of behaviour that I would much rather remained a closely guarded family secret. It's when somebody else is present to see that she only eats two peas and a tomato for her dinner, or that she's rampaging around with a chocolate-smeared face when she should be sleeping peacefully that it's brought home to me that, if I am working on it, I'm obviously not working hard enough. I might try to pretend to myself and others that this is just a one-off and make lame excuses about her being a little bit over-excited and she's not usually like this but I am forced reluctantly to face my own shortcomings and hers. Grimly I decide that things are going to change around here. Again.

So much for my problems, which seem to me to be incredibly difficult to solve. She has her problems too, which usually seem to me to be incredibly easy to solve – but not as far as she's concerned. The term 'drama queen' has more than once crossed my mind, and my lips. If I can be guilty of making mountains out of molehills, she can make entire Himalayan ranges out of a hole in the ground. There's no point in explaining to her that she doesn't actually *have* any problems, that she only has to wait a few years and *then* she'll know what problems are. A corner torn off a picture that she was drawing can be the cue for loud laments and demands that I fix it *immediately*. I once made the mistake of remarking brightly that there is no problem that can't be solved, and she took me at my word. She creates problems and I have to do something about them. Most of the time sellotape, sewing kits or screwdrivers can come to the rescue if the damage isn't too great. When she dropped her favourite bracelet down the plughole it was possible to unscrew the U-bend to retrieve it; when it went down a gap in the floorboards a cunning arrangement of wire coat hanger and magnet did the trick. (Although I did manage to find an undiscoverable hiding place for it after that.) She has a touching faith in her parents' ability to fix things, and much as she thinks that pink medicine will cure everything, she thinks that a china cup that has been smashed to smithereens just needs a dab of glue to make it good as new. Sometimes an irretrievably demolished toy is a problem solved in itself as far as I'm concerned ('Thank God we've seen the back of that one'), but she rarely sees it my way.

If I do manage to convince her that things don't last forever (especially when dropped from a great height) and what the hell does she think the dustbin is *for*, she will fall back on her other problem-solving technique: 'Oh well, we can always buy a new one.' We? *We*? What's this 'We'? Since when did you start paying for breakages? She still thinks that money comes from a machine in the wall, and when you run out you simply go and get some more. It's bad enough when she's planning a replacement purchase for a headless Barbie, but when she starts applying it to the car, which she has just scraped down the side with her scooter, it just goes to highlight the different ways in which we perceive problems.

Her sense of proportion is sometimes seriously awry. If I hear the urgent cry: 'Mummy, I've got a problem here' I can rush into the room to find anything from a radiator accidentally wrenched off the wall to a loose thread on her skirt. She doesn't distinguish between a major incident and a minor irritation. Making a little mistake in a picture, birthday card or homework can turn into a massive trauma. The tentative suggestion: 'Why don't you just do it again?'

isn't nearly good enough. She may get into the mood when a pencil line in the wrong place can cause her to go into what her father calls her 'Russian actress' mode: back of the hand to the forehead, accompanied by loud, dry sobs and an expression of such unremitting tragedy it immediately makes us laugh. Parental guffawing is like a red rag to a bull, of course, so we have to wipe the smiles off our faces and go into long and patient explanations about how everybody makes mistakes and sometimes things turn out *better* the second time you do them, while getting amused and irritated by turns. And yet the fact that she's made a dirty great stain with shampoo in the middle of a practically brand-new stair carpet is absolutely no cause for concern. I suppose she thinks we can just buy another one.

Perhaps her inability to understand the word 'problem' is a good thing. It simply shows that she really doesn't know what it means and in her world the application of sellotape to a torn picture, the logistics of getting to two parties on the same day or how to cope with the loss of a favourite outgrown T-shirt are about as problematical as it gets. Especially when she has parents on hand, ever ready with the Araldite and apparently ever-open wallets. She is busily planning a new room and her next holiday. How we are going to pay for it all is our problem – that's what we are there for.

Although our daughter might think we are Mr and Mrs

Fixit, where I'm concerned she's being remarkably generous. What I would do if we really encountered any major problems I don't much like to dwell on. No point in worrying about things before they happen, is there? (This, from the woman who spent serious mind-time imagining a twenty-stone daughter drinking only from a baby cup – just because she wanted a ride in the buggy.) Looking at my past record, however, it has become clear how I would deal with it if we were hit by any major complication. So far I have left problems to sort themselves out; I have hit on solutions quite by accident; and I have relied on the chance intervention of others. My daughter will ignore me but take instruction from her peer group, her teacher, slight acquaintances and the cat. The solution to any future problem is obvious: I'll get somebody else to sort it out. Friends, relatives, neighbours and people I see at bus stops all have their instructions and I've already enrolled the cat on a course in child psychology. I foresee no major problems there.

Chapter Sixteen

Worn-out genes

SHOULD WE IN FUTURE BE CALLED INTO THE head teacher's office because our daughter has been displaying criminal tendencies we could just deny all parental responsibility and blame heredity. God knows what is lying in the murky depths of her gene pool – we may feel as if we've been around since the Flood, but neither of us has traced our family history back too far, which is probably just as well. If any of my forebears finished up at the end of a rope I think I'd rather not know about it. We like to think of her as our daughter, but she is, as is everyone, the product of hundreds of thousands of years of (presumably) human liaisons – some of them more dangerous than others. Spooky.

When she was born I was incredibly proud of what we had produced between us. What a clever pair we were! Gratifyingly, everyone else agreed with us and immediately did what everyone does when a new baby arrives: they started looking for family likenesses. Opinion was pretty well evenly divided between her striking resemblance to either her mum or her dad. Frankly, I couldn't see it myself. I thought she looked more like a coconut (a gorgeous coconut) than she did either of us, but people still insisted on discerning strong similarities between eyes and noses and ears. Even I was influenced by all this speculation and started squinting at this tiny little scrap, hoping against hope that she didn't have her grandfather's nose. Have you ever seen a small baby with a large and distinctive nose? No, neither have I, but it didn't stop me from imagining I could detect something of the Roman in her tiny little button hooter. Lots of people claimed she was the image of her father (about the same number who saw her as the dead spit of her mother), which was a little disconcerting. Only because I had read in *Practical Makeup for the Stage* by T. W. Bamford (published 1946) that: 'The pure Slav is very distinctive, and is anything but a classic type. There is something primitive in the facial cast, and the general expression of sullen, smouldering moroseness adds to this effect.' Thank God she wasn't pure, in that case. But fresh from the hospital she really just looked like a baby, and it was only when I looked at the photographs a couple of years later that I realised that, not only did she not resemble either of us, she wasn't even the gorgeous creation that I thought I had brought home. She was just a little baby with a lot of growing to do. It's quite some time before newborns develop that look of smouldering moroseness.

It was while all this controversy was raging over her unformed features that I was told about the theory that babies always look like their fathers. This is apparently a defence mechanism against Mr Neanderthal suspecting Mrs Neanderthal of playing the field and throwing Mrs Neanderthal and her ginger-haired cuckoo out of the connubial cave. This makes sense, unless Mrs Neanderthal *has* been playing the field, which I imagine wasn't unheard of, even if it wasn't much of a field to play in. Surely the roving Mrs Neanderthal would be on very shaky ground if babies were unmistakably their fathers' sons or daughters, and as it is *Mother* Nature who regulates these things, I would have thought that she would give her girls a fighting chance. Far more sensible for them to come into the world as featureless blobs that you can pass off as anybody's offspring – plus it gives their relatives something to argue about over the teacups and muslin squares.

But it doesn't take long for that squashed, brand-new look to even itself out and within a couple of months our daughter looked like herself. As she grew, she certainly didn't look like me, as I was constantly reminded whenever I lifted her up and caught sight of our faces side by side in the mirror. You'll never do yourself any favours by comparing skin tones with a two-year-old, but that cruel reflection often made me wonder whether we were even the same species, let alone mother and daughter. I was certain of one thing: we were never going to be taken for sisters. So it came as a bit of a shock, when she was about four, to find that although I could see no similarity between this lovely little girl and her middle-aged old bat of a mother, that she looked *exactly* like the photographs of me at that age. This threw up all sorts of conflicting emotions. I was pleased that there was such a strong resemblance after all – I wouldn't like people to think I had stolen her, even if I had to carry around a photograph of myself to prove it. But if the four-year-old mother and daughter were so similar, was the connection going to run in parallel as she grew? Was she also going to suffer braces on her teeth, impossible hair and stockings full of old hockey muscles in later life? Should I start warning her now about the importance of doing stomach curls and paying attention to moisturising elbows, knees and heels? Was it too soon to start her on a relationship with a hairdresser she could trust? How long was she going to keep that perfect skin? I was pleased that she looked like me, horrified that she might turn into me. Surely my girl deserved better than *this*?

What else had she inherited from me, I wondered? Perhaps some nasty little character traits that I would prefer to be buried with me, not perpetuated in another human being. When I noticed her pouting with concentration, I could see not only myself, but my brother too. She puts off doing things she doesn't want to, as well. Is that because she has my blood running through her veins, or because she's only little and life is supposed to be fun? If I detected signs of her mother's laziness developing, would I be able to nip it in the bud and change her into a go-getter, or is it stamped forever into her neurons? Would I have any influence at all on the sort of person she grew into, or was I fighting a losing battle against the legions of her ancestors?

As her character formed I watched closely to see what it would form into, and had a very bad moment once when it occurred to me that she might not be very nice. On reflection, my fears were probably caused by the fact that she was about two at the time, when human beings do tend to display some rather nasty characteristics, especially towards their parents. Once, a spectacular show of temper caused both me and her father to stare helplessly at each other and at the tiny little ball of wrath and say 'Where did *that* come from?' Her father concluded gloomily, 'I think she's got my mother's temper.' That hadn't occurred to me – the fact that her family extended beyond her two parents. There was I, busily comparing my gestures and facial tics to my daughter's, when it was possible that she was heir to the characteristics of somebody who died before she was born. I, too, was born after the death of one of my grandmothers, and it gives me a little *Twilight Zone* shiver if my mother claims I share some characteristics with a woman I never even met. This was a whole new can of worms for me to open and dig about in. My daughter could have spent her time in the womb trawling through previous generations and doing a sort of pick'n'mix with her heritage. After some fruitless speculation, it proved rather too large a concept for me to grasp, and I'm a little hazy on the mechanics of genetics anyway. How much do you really inherit from your relations? And how far back do you have to go to become totally removed from them? Do the genes of a twelfth-century mass murderer get watered down over the years or do they flare up again in later generations? If, after a particularly fraught day, I deny her as my daughter and claim that she is in fact the spawn of Satan, is her bad behaviour due to the fact that one of her ancestors was a gibbet-swinger, or is it because she has a cold coming on? Whose characteristics has she chosen to inherit? Perhaps she will reap the benefit of a musical great-uncle, but escape the hatchet-faced grimness of her great-great-grandmother. The more I looked at her family tree, the more it resembled a dark and tangled forest, and I couldn't believe that all this jumble of history was combined in one small girl.

But it isn't, of course. Once I'd stopped trying to piece together an Identikit picture assembled from various branches of the family I realised that I wasn't really being fair to her. She is not a walking jigsaw of different family features, she is more than the sum of her parts. I don't see myself as lots of bits of other people rolled into one, so why should I regard her in that way? It might have been interesting to poke about among photographs of long-dead relatives and wonder at the vast network of familial relationships that led to her existence, but it didn't do to read too much into it. I still fret that I may have cursed her with a lifetime of unmanageable hair, but at least I don't seem to have passed on my pathological dread of hairdressers, so it's a kink in her genealogy that she may be able to iron out – with professional help.

It would be more sensible to stop worrying about recessive genes and evildoing ancestors and concentrate on the powerful influence of nurture over nature. The extended family she had been born into might very well have given her the gift of short legs and long sight, or a short temper and long pockets – we'd just have to wait and see. Meanwhile, I had no excuse to just shrug my shoulders and claim I had no control if she had inherited a nose-picking gene, or the gene that determines how quickly you can choose your clothes in the morning. I had a feeling any head teacher wouldn't buy it, either. Nurture can fight against nature or enhance it, but whatever battles were to be fought, her home environment was going to go a long way towards forming her character and her interests. I could teach her so much! Apart from moral values, tolerance, fortitude, kindness and civic responsibility (not spitting in the street) there was a whole world of literature, art, film and theatre to which I could open her eyes. School can't cover everything, and I could introduce her to the Greek myths, grammar, Gauguin and *The Great Gatsby*! No sooner will she stop banging on a tin drum than she's going to be reading it. Just think! She doesn't yet know what happens at the end of *Rebecca*! What a treat there is in store for her, to read it for the first time! She doesn't yet know what happens to Anna Karenina, Madame Bovary or Trilby! They all die, unfortunately, but that's not the point. She was going to enter into my world, have her mind expanded, ditch this ridiculous liking for the Cheeky Girls. She *shall* enjoy films with subtitles if it bloody well kills me.

In the middle of all my elaborate brainwashing plans a niggling worry pulled me up short. Suppose she develops an interest in physics? Or maths? Or, God forbid, *football*? I was selfishly hoping to turn her into a little carbon copy of myself, with the same attitudes and interests, but there would be no point in me casually leaving copies of Dickens and Thackeray lying around if what she really wanted to read was a Manchester United fanzine or the periodic table (the real one, not the Primo Levi version). Could I rely on the influence of home life or is there a nineteenth-century novel gene that she might have missed out on? If she veered off in another direction, how could I possibly hope to connect with a mathematician or an engineer? What would we talk about if her mind was on a higher plane – or a lower one? I could just imagine her impatiently trying to explain the beauty of a mathematical construct, or the offside rule, to her idiot mother who was mired in the namby-pamby world of books and pictures. Never mind criminal genes, suppose she surprised us all by reverting to an alchemist ancestor? What do nuclear physicists do when their children become circus performers? Applaud their achievements, one would hope, but I bet even they aren't above scattering copies of the *New Scientist* around the Big Top, like religious tracts. Would I still be trying to get her interested in Jane Austen when she turned into a professional snowboarder?

All this happened before she could even read her own name, let alone *Finnegans Wake*, so I had absolutely nothing on which to base all these hypothetical musings. Oh well, I thought gloomily, whatever she turns out to be interested in, at least I can teach her not to spit in the street. And with a bit of luck we might share the same taste in soft furnishings – always a good topic for conversation. I just hope she forgives me for the hair.

There was really no point in indulging in all this aimless conjecture (which didn't stop me doing it, of course). Family is family and she was stuck with whatever we might or might not have given her through the bloodline. A lot of families have skeletons in the cupboard. Even more have living, breathing, fully-fleshed embarrassments who not only refuse to stay in the cupboard but insist on walking about in broad daylight and inviting themselves for Christmas dinner. There's nothing I can do about her kith and kin, but luckily, so far she seems quite happy with what fate has dealt her in the way of relations, although it took her a little while to work out even the simplest of family ties.

Once we had established that no, Mummy and Daddy didn't go to the same school and we weren't even brought up in the same country, let alone street, she got the hang of the idea that people can meet when they are adults and then have a daughter, you don't actually have to be betrothed at birth. She went through a short phase of wanting to marry me, and her father, and the cat, because she loved us all equally and it seemed the logical conclusion. When that puzzle was sorted out she progressed to other members of the family and tried valiantly to see how we were all related. She thought it was terribly funny when she made the first connection: 'So you're *my* mummy and Nanny is *your* mummy! Ha ha!' and there was much discussion about mummies and tummies and the astonishing fact that I was once a baby and a small girl. 'Yes, dear, I know it doesn't seem possible, thanks for reminding me.' And as she only has one mother and one grandmother, it logically followed that she could only have one aunt. 'She can't be my aunt, I've already got one.' 'You've got *loads* of aunts!' While reeling off by name the flocks of her sainted aunts I also included in the bona fide list people like my niece (who is technically a cousin) and her father's cousin's wife. (Who is technically – I don't know what. A second aunt? Who cares – if it walks like an aunt and quacks like an aunt, it must be an aunt.)

What I was careful not to do was to lumber friends and neighbours with the handle 'auntie' or 'uncle'. I was well into my thirties before I could stop thinking of the neighbours of my childhood as 'Auntie Phil and Uncle Tom' and when I was a teenager I don't think I called them anything at all. My adolescent self-esteem couldn't cope with 'Auntie and Uncle' but it just seemed far too rude to refer to them bluntly as Phil and Tom. So my daughter is on first-name terms with my friends and her relations, a habit which has spread through- out our family. When my niece's boy thought it funny to address me as 'Auntie Kate' I was quick to remind him that 'I'm not your Auntie Kate, I'm your Great-Aunt Kathryn and I'll thank you to remember that, you little blister.' Even though I was joking, as soon as the phrase 'Great-Aunt Kathryn' passed my lips I could feel myself shrinking into a withered old crone. We stuck to 'Kate' after that. I like to think I'm quite sprightly for my age.

If there are a few pretenders to the title of 'aunt' or 'uncle', 'cousin' can cover just about anything. I haven't sat my daughter down with a pencil and paper and sketched out a family tree as I don't think I have a piece of paper big enough, and I use 'cousin' in the Shakespearean sense of 'practically anybody, really'. Her favourite cousins, those closest to her in age, are actually second cousins (I think), as is the previously unknown set of boys we found in a small village in the Czech Republic. Even her father didn't know of their existence, as he hadn't seen his own cousins for years, and it was quite an odd feeling to see her sitting across a table from complete strangers with whom she had quite close blood ties. I'm sure my long-lost cousins had children too, so she'd be related to them as well if I ever found them. The world is swarming with cousins who have been removed once, twice, a hundred times – some of them never to be put back to where they had been removed from. Somewhere out there my father's brother's son's son is unaware that he is a close relative of my daughter: it's all just too, too weird. She's got relations a-go-go – I hope they won't all want to turn up for her wedding.

But what she hasn't got, of course, is brothers and sisters. She makes a point of reminding me of this at regular intervals, which makes me feel terrific, of course. It's no good me telling her that she'll always have her own room, never have to wear hand-me-downs, never have to look after a much-hated younger brother or sister or share her toys. She has no concept of sibling rivalry, she just thinks she would always have somebody to play with. I can't explain to her the cruelty of timing, and am just left with the guilty feeling that I have, through no fault of my own, deprived her of the one thing that would make her happy throughout life. It's not as if we *planned* it this way. So, barring a miracle, our daughter is destined to remain without a little sibling to boss around. She'll have to make do with her mum and dad – and the rest of her family.

Or should I say 'families'. In the making of any baby there are (preferably) two families involved, although you wouldn't think so sometimes. Any traditional wedding should give us a clue as to what's in store for the product of any union. Are you with the bride or the groom? Distaff or spear side? A distaff represents the feminine pursuit of spinning, but I've no doubt it, too, could be used as a weapon. There's a lot to be said for having the two sides of our daughter's family firmly located in different countries, because they each claim her as their own, and should they ever meet I dare say the lack of a common language wouldn't stop them from arguing about her.

Apart from in certain rural communities, a close-knit family is generally agreed to be a good thing. Chain-mail woven close enough to repel all attempts to infiltrate might not be such a bright idea. We're supposed to get on our bikes and extend the gene pool, according to geneticists. 'Try everything once except folk dancing and incest' is a pretty solid rule for life, so when two families come together and result in a third, it should be cause for rejoicing. Do they mingle? Do they interact? They are more likely to ignore each other's existence. My family seem quite capable of blotting from their minds the fact that our daughter is half Czech. Her father's side of the family talk a lot about summer camps in Bohemia and hate to acknowledge that we actually live in London. I'm sure the same would have happened if her father and I had been brought up in the same street. Why are there so many in-law jokes? Because 'blood is thicker than water' and families, no matter how much they might bicker and fight within their own walls, have a habit of clinging together against the enemy. The enemy is classed as any blow-in, infiltrator or anybody who isn't a direct descendant of your own precious clan. 'She's only related by *marriage*' is something you hear quite often about a bothersome relation, and I have no doubt that should we live to see our daughter settled with a life partner, whoever it is won't be good enough.

Families. Huh. Can't live with them, can't exist without them. I like being part of a family, but it can't be denied that each and every one of us at some time has wished that you *could* choose your relations. It first struck me when I was quite a young child and I found out that I had been born at home. It was terrible news. It meant that there was absolutely no possibility of me having been swapped at birth, so all my fantasies about being in reality a princess or a fairy or even just a little bit more interesting crumbled to dust. I was stuck with this rather ordinary family with no aristocratic or magical connections. No romantic family of Romanies was going to turn up and claim me as their own, I would never be crowned queen of a distant country and, moreover, if these two people who claimed to be my parents were telling the truth there was also precious little chance of me growing up to be tall. I've had plenty of time since to get used to it, but it came as a great blow at the time. Our daughter has not yet reached the stage of shouting that she never asked to be born, or generally blaming us for not being rich, glamorous or somebody else's parents, but I suppose it's just a matter of time. I can't remember what age I was when the scales fell from my eyes, so I'm not sure how long I've got before she starts judging us, comparing us with other parents and finding us wanting. Because it is inevitable, isn't it? When we come under her close scrutiny it's not likely that she will reflect how lucky she is to have been born into the best family in the world. So she will be just as ensnared by the tangled lines of her lineage as the rest of us, and she'll have to put up with it, just like the rest of us.

And meanwhile, she'll also have to put up with living inside this particular nuclear family. All those labyrinthine bloodlines have led to these three people, living in the same house, with all the troubles that brings. If home is the place where they have to let you in, is your family your constant help and support, or the root of all your problems? I think we have a perfectly normal, conventional existence, but we are living the sort of family life that can be blamed for practically every evil in the world. That's *including* floods and famine because we are wasteful westerners who probably notch up another degree of global warming every time we switch on a light or put the rubbish out. Not to mention all the resentments, neuroses, bitterness and regret that I am saddling my daughter with every time I get cross with her or make a joke at her expense. When I think I am creating a close and loving family home, am I in fact imprisoning my daughter in a claustrophobic relationship with over-protective parents who don't understand her need for freedom and privacy? Actually, I think I'm creating a close and loving family home, and Freud can go hang, but I have a nasty suspicion that I will only find out what a repressive, uncaring, selfish mother I am when our daughter hits teenagehood. As they say, even in the best-regulated families, blood will out. I just hope it doesn't stain the carpets too much.

Chapter Seventeen

Putting the 'lark' into Larkin

SO HERE I AM, WITH A HOUSE, A MORTGAGE, AN
overdraft, a husband, a daughter, an au pair and a cat.
It would only take a Labrador and a four-wheel drive for me
to have become everything I heartily despised when I was
a teenager. I am Mrs Conventionality. I would rather go to a
garden centre than a clothes shop. I don't like staying up
late, or loud music, or plastic beer glasses. I don't actually
worry about limescale, but I do think about it quite a lot. I
like to redecorate when the paintwork gets grubby, and I
almost believe that I can transform my living room with a
couple of luxury throws and 'clever use of lighting'. I would
have to be lavishly bribed to wear high heels and I think
sexy underwear is a shocking waste of money. Jumping into
the fountains in Trafalgar Square is not an amusing and

spontaneous action, it is puerile and insanitary. If forced to do it at gunpoint I would probably take my watch off first. I have no desire to indulge in extreme sports, or push myself to the limit or appear on reality TV. I have strong opinions on the importance of teaching grammar. Pop music is boring and repetitive and the singers don't wear enough clothes. Let's face it, I'm a walking cliché: not only have I become a mother, but I think I have become mine.

What happened to my plans for travelling the world, meeting fascinating people and living in a Parisian atelier? Where is the glamour and excitement? I was going to live my life like a Bohemian – instead I ended up marrying one. He does a lot of DIY and to my certain knowledge has never written a line of poetry or worn a floppy hat. Bohemians aren't supposed to flick through the Ikea catalogue or buy bulb planters. They're supposed to live lives free of clocks and timetables, drink absinthe and talk into the small hours about art and literature – not complain about London Transport before going to bed at half past ten. Instead of a carefree existence filled with colour and adventure, we have in fact turned into our own parents. Did I want all this? Didn't I want a tepee and a cannabis crop, not a mortgage and bedding plants?

No, of course I didn't. I may have had some vague teenage notions about 'finding myself' but it wasn't long before I realised that I was there all the time and I didn't have to go to Marrakesh to discover my true identity. My true identity may have had a few daydreams about a fabulous, free and fun nonconformist lifestyle but it was also rather partial to square meals and a comfortable bed to sleep in. Once I had sown my wild oats I was quite prepared to harvest them and make a nourishing oat-based snack.

Standing on a train on a wet Monday in November is enough to rekindle that hankering after colour and adventure, then I remember that I do know someone who was brought up in Paris between the wars in real Bohemian fashion. The daughter of artist parents, her childhood was filled with painters, writers, dancers and actors. She drops names like a waiter drops plates. She has sat on Picasso's knee! When I first made her acquaintance I was dazzled by her glamorous and fascinating life and regretted my humdrum existence. Why had I never done anything interesting? Why did I have no stories to tell? But glamour is often only a naked lightbulb away from tawdriness. After knowing her for a while I caught myself thinking, 'If she tells that bloody Picasso story again I swear I shall bite her.' One afternoon we were sitting in her garden drinking wine from elegant black-stemmed glasses. It was only after a few sips that I realised the stems weren't black, they were *hollow*. I don't know whether it was the thought of the centuries of dirt that my wine had been filtered through, or the years of middle-class upbringing that caused the bile to rise to my throat, but I suddenly thought, 'Oh, bugger Bohemians, give me Fairy Liquid and a bottle brush.'

So it's not really surprising that I sound exactly like my father when I'm fulminating against the improper use of the apostrophe, or that I still use my mother's method of cleaning windows. I was never destined to live among impoverished painters or freedom-loving travellers, I was destined to do pretty much what my parents did. Get a job, settle down, build a rockery – all the usual stuff that people do. If I had ever thought about it I would have known that I would lead a life that wasn't so very different from the one I was brought up in. Except in one important respect. (Well, two, if you count the rockery.) When it comes to bringing up children, we will never become carbon copies of our parents, because we know better. With their rather poor example before us we can't help but do a better job of it than they did.

Once I became a parent myself the guilt about what I had done to them as a child struck me rather forcefully. They weren't old after all – they were just prematurely aged with all the worry we caused them! That soon wore off, however, and I was able to forgive myself for once being a teenager. I didn't ask to be born, did I? No, I might choose to plant the same shrubs as my parents, but I was never going to become like them. I would never perpetuate their mistakes, humiliate my daughter by telling hilarious stories about her toilet training to anyone who would listen, make her kiss mustachioed aunts or ignore her urgent requests for attention. We would be open and honest parents, there would be no family secrets whispered behind closed doors away from little pitchers (except *that* secret, of course, but she's only related by marriage) and our daughter would be consulted on our plans and her opinions considered. Moreover, we were going to remain proper people in our own right. Our daughter would understand that we were an interesting and amusing couple with a wide circle of inter-esting and amusing friends – not like that collection of excruciating bores that our parents inflicted on us. Of course our daughter would like our friends as much as we do, and not regard them as the tedious relics of a bygone age that clutter up the house every so often and ask her how she's doing at school. I will never watch *Top of the Pops* with pursed lips and then maintain (against all available evidence) that at least you could understand the words in my day. I will never comment on current fashion with the claims 'I used to wear things like that when I was a girl,' or 'You could make that for half the price.' My husband begs me to shoot him if he ever starts telling the same stories over and over again like his father did. We're both quite adamant about it: we will never make the same mistakes as our parents did, and we will never become like them.

Anyway, parenting is different now. As well as having

become a verb (when did *that* happen?), it's much more relaxed and much more informed. Children are included more, consulted more (and consequently ignored, but you do feel obliged to at least ask their opinions) and generally treated more like human beings and less like troublesome homunculi. So our daughter is unlikely to suffer the same embarrassments, humiliations and resentments as we did because it's all changed now and we are bound to make a far better fist of it than our poor ill-equipped parents. It's obvious to us, although strangely our parents singularly fail to see it that way, and have consistently refused to admit our superiority in the child-rearing stakes. Former generations ought to be full of people smacking their foreheads instead of their children and saying 'Of *course*! How wrong we were to make you eat everything on your plate. Your way is so much better.' But it doesn't happen, for some reason. Anyway, that's their problem, not ours. It's of no consequence that my mother obviously thinks my daughter is over-indulged and has far too much stuff and that I should put my foot down harder and more often. She's my daughter and I think I know best how to look after her.

And yet before me I can see a future shade of a fully grown girl saying things like:

'Yes, Dad, you *have* told me about the first time
you bought a car', *or*

'No, I can't say I do regard David Bowie as
Britain's finest contribution to pop music', *or*:

'Actually I always hated all those dance classes
you made me go to', *or* – worst of all,

'She's my daughter and I think I know best how to
look after her.'

It's a vision I can't dispel and I don't know how I'm going
to stop it from becoming a self-fulfilling prophecy. I may have
stopped myself from whispering with a martyred air, 'Not
now, dear, Mummy's tired' but I have substituted my own
version: 'Leave me alone, I'm knackered.' Given a similar
set of circumstances to those of my own childhood I would
probably have no compunction in dismissing my daughter's
objections to an unpleasant chore with the words, 'Yes, I
know she's got prickles on her face, but she's family.' And
it doesn't stop there. Not only will we make exactly the
same mistakes as our parents, but we, the parents of the new
millennium, will also find far more ingenious and novel ways
of sending our daughter into therapy. I shall probably find
out that a relaxed and liberal upbringing results in her
having a problem with authority and the inability to hold
down a job. My reluctance to be a martinet will end in me
having to support a sulky and bitter layabout to the end of
my days. You never know, it could happen.

You can't escape destiny, and my destiny seems to be predictable and not a little dull. So, has becoming a mother taught me anything at *all*, apart from the fact that I apparently have a really peculiar way of tying shoelaces? I've learned that pregnancy-induced daydreams are best shelved when reality in the form of a baby hits home, and that nothing much goes as planned. Instead of making ill-informed decisions and impossible-to-keep rules and formulating half-baked theories I've found a way of playing it by ear and trying to catch anything that life throws at me. I never say 'never' but also try to avoid saying 'we'll see.' Children aren't as stupid as we would like to think and immediately recognise the true meaning of this phrase as: 'I can't think of a reason why not at the moment but as soon as I do I'll just say "no".' With this in mind I try to remember what it was like to be a child and not throw a fit when I find that somebody has filled the watering can with dead leaves. I've learned that the real purpose of a mother is always to carry a large bag containing everything that might possibly be needed at any time. And that when something is needed it is always at the bottom of that bag under a pile of dirty wet wipes and sticky sweet wrappers. It didn't take the birth of a child to make me realise my limitations – just walking about in the world for a few years did that – but if anything it has taught me that my limits actually take quite a long time to reach. I now know what it really means to be tired and anxious and wrathful and frustrated in ways that I never did before I became a mother. And I've also learned to put up with it.

So what with all the guilt, self-loathing, frustration and despair that dog my days you might think that I would give myself up as a bad case and hope that my daughter will find a way of rearing herself without me fucking it all up for her. But despite my obvious lack of perfection – even comp-etence in some areas – I don't honestly think I do too badly. I've decided that Philip Larkin got it wrong. When he wrote 'They fuck you up, your mum and dad. They may not mean to, but they do.' he didn't take into account that, even if they don't mean to, they bring you up as well. I might hand on a modicum of misery to my daughter, but I'll hand on some quite useful stuff as well. She'll always know the correct use of the apostrophe, for example. I have plenty of bad moments when I wonder what the hell I'm doing, and I don't need laughing boy Larkin to tell me it's a tough job, but I simply refuse to believe that bringing up a child is a licence to crush a psyche.

Against all the odds, I'm optimistic. My outlook on life tends more towards Pop Larkin than Philip. The responsi-bility of being a parent, the constant anxieties, self-doubt and glaring errors should be enough to crush me under the weight of my own incompetence, but – wouldn't you know it – no such thing has happened. At no point has my daughter been forced to take things into her own hands because her mother has finally lost all grip on reality. At no point have I seriously thought 'I can't do this, it's too hard.' Not only does the muddling through and making things up as we go along seem to be working – a good part of it is actually fun. We worry, we read articles by child psychologists, scour problem pages and have earnest discussions about whether we're doing the right things – and it all achieves less than a good old tickling session. If parenthood is mainly busking it, I reckon my hat contains a pretty tidy sum.

So, despite the dizzyingly rapid rate of change over the last few years, my job has barely begun and the next few years will probably hold as many pitfalls for me as I've managed to clamber out of over the last few years. Spots and SATs are still to come, and there will be more challenges for me, too. If I've managed to teach somebody how to progress from nappy to toilet, how difficult can it be to explain some other basic bodily functions? Very, I suspect. How will I cope when the girl who loved me starts to judge me? Very badly, I suspect. How will I help her with her maths homework? Very, *very* badly, I suspect. (No, I don't suspect, I know.) I can't promise that I'll ever get any better at being a mother, but I shall try to do my best, knowing that it will never be good enough and learning to live with my inadequacies.

So, Anna, the light of my life and the star of my show – I'm your mother and you also will have to live with my inadequacies. If you can keep on loving me, try not to judge me too harshly and find it in your heart to forgive me, I'm sure you'll do fine. In spite of, not because of, the efforts of your mother.

Vermilion books are available from all good bookshops or by ordering direct on 01624 677237. Or visit our website at www.randomhouse.co.uk